M000230149

TRUE CRIME CASE HISTORIES

VOLUME 10

JASON NEAL

IDIGITAL GROUP

Cover images of:

Ricky Riffe: (top-left)

Mary Rowles: (top-right)

Ezra McCandless: (bottom-left)

Frank Jarvis Atwood: (bottom-right)

More books by Jason Neal

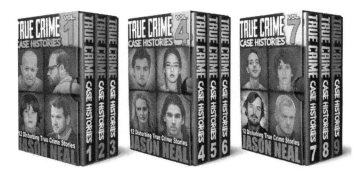

Looking for more?? I am constantly adding new volumes of True Crime Case Histories. The series **can be read in any order,** and all books are available in paperback, hardcover, and audiobook.

Check out the complete series at:

https://amazon.com/author/jason-neal

All Jason Neal books are also available in **AudioBook format at Audible.com.** Enjoy a **Free Audiobook** when you signup for a 30-Day trial using this link:

https://geni.us/AudibleTrueCrime

FREE BONUS EBOOK FOR MY READERS

As my way of saying "Thank you" for downloading, I'm giving away a FREE True Crime e-book I think you'll enjoy.

https://TrueCrimeCaseHistories.com

Just visit the link above to let me know where to send your free book!

CONTENTS

INTRODUCTION

True crime is not for everyone. But chances are, if you've picked up this book, you already know that. Actual true crime is not like watching an episode of CSI. Even television true crime documentaries can skim over the sticky details. Real true crime can be unsettling for many people. However, I do my best not to leave out any details in my books. My intention isn't to shock but rather to give the reader a glimpse into the killer's mind. I don't begin to think that I can understand the mind of a diabolical monster, but I can guarantee that curiosity will keep us turning pages and endlessly searching for answers.

Each story in my books requires hours of tedious research. I search through court records, old newspaper articles, police records, autopsy reports, and first-hand accounts. Although I may occasionally change a character's name or fictionalize bits of dialogue, these crimes really happened to real people. Sadly, this is the world in which we live.

As always, I ask a favor of my readers. I continuously try to find true crime stories that aren't already all over the

Internet or covered by true crime documentaries. That's why I ask my readers to send me story ideas.

Some of the most interesting stories in my previous books are ones my readers have sent to me. Many are cases that have almost no nationwide coverage – stories from small towns that the rest of the world has forgotten. I thrive on researching stories like these and ask my readers to send them my way. If you have a story like this, email me and I'll do my best to find as much info as possible so I can include it in a future volume. Readers like you have submitted several of the story ideas contained in this volume.

———

Lastly, please join my mailing list for discounts, updates, and a free book. You can sign up for that at

TrueCrimeCaseHistories.com

Additional photos, videos, and documents pertaining to the cases in this volume can be found on the accompanying web page at:

http://TrueCrimeCaseHistories.com/vol10/

Thanks again for reading and I sincerely hope you gain some insight from this volume of True Crime Case Histories.

- Jason Neal

CHAPTER 1
A SAD HOLIDAY SEASON

November 25, 2000, was like any other rainy winter Saturday in Leeds, England. Sixteen-year-old Leanne Tiernan and her best friend, Sarah Whitehouse, spent the day shopping for Christmas presents for their friends and family.

The sun set early in Northern England in November and it was already dark when they boarded the bus home. The girls got off their bus at Houghley Lane at 4:50, said their goodbyes, and walked in opposite directions home. Sarah watched as Leanne walked toward Houghley Gill, a shortcut to her home with an unlit path leading through a dark, wooded area.

When Sarah arrived home, she called Leanne's home but was surprised that she hadn't made it back yet. They were both an equal distance from their homes and she'd had plenty of time to make it back. Leanne's mother, Sharon, called her cell phone but there was no answer. When she tried to call again, the phone rang four times before it cut off entirely.

Leanne's mother called the police and a search started immediately. Several branches of law enforcement searched the
area around Houghley Gill while friends and family
members gathered volunteers to help. Sharon had a sinking
feeling that if her daughter didn't come home by 10:00 p.m.,
she would never return.

Leanne didn't return that night and the missing person
investigation dragged on for weeks. There was simply no
sign of Leanne Tiernan. Police searched more than 1,400
houses, 800 sheds, garages, and outbuildings, and more than
150 businesses throughout the neighborhood, but they found
no clues whatsoever. Investigators questioned 140 men in
the area and twelve search warrants were issued.

Police dive teams drained and scoured three miles of canals.
Utility companies searched abandoned drains and drain
shafts. Police suspended garbage collection so officers could
search dumpsters throughout the area, but there was still no
trace of Leanne.

On December 3, television news crews recreated the last
movements of Sarah and Leanne. Sarah played herself and
Leanne was performed by her sister, Michelle. She wore the
same clothes that Leanne wore the night she went missing.
Leanne's face was displayed on milk cartons and a local businessman offered a reward of £10,000 for her safe return.

There were many calls to the police but only one lead
provided any helpful clues. After seeing the television reen-
actment, a woman came forward to say that she had seen a
man in Houghley Gill around the same time Leanne went
missing. The man was walking a black and tan dog.

She described the man as approximately five feet eight inches
tall, with a stocky build and a round, reddish, possibly-

scarred face. He wore a three-quarter-length waterproof jacket, dirty jeans, and a black stocking cap.

Police tracked down seventy men who walked dogs in that area and showed them to the woman, but none of the men were the one she saw that day and all were eliminated as suspects.

Police generated a composite drawing of the man and released it to the public, but almost ten months had passed and detectives were no closer to finding Leanne.

Leanne's family members had all but given up hope. Reluctantly, they resorted to combing through red-light districts in the area, thinking the fifteen-year-old may have been lured into a life of prostitution.

Sixteen miles from where Leanne went missing, Mark Bissen was walking his two dogs through Lindley Wood, an area of deep forest in North Yorkshire near Otley, when he came across an object in the woods. It looked like a package bound in twine. However, when he saw a sock nearby, he knew it wasn't a package. There was a body inside.

When police arrived, they found an object wrapped in a floral-printed duvet cover held together by black twine. Inside the duvet was the body of Leanne Tiernan, wrapped in nine large, green trash bags. A black garbage bag was around her head, held tightly by a dark-colored scarf, a leather dog collar, and a plastic cable tie. She had died from strangulation.

Her arms were bound behind her back with three plastic cable ties – one around each wrist and a third securing the other two together.

She was still wearing the clothes she had disappeared in except for her coat and boots, which were missing.

Strangely, after ten months, the body was very much intact. Decomposition was minimal and they were able to identify her as Leanne through fingerprints. After analyzing her body tissue, forensic investigators determined she had been frozen. This explained the lack of decomposition and the fact that animals had not torn at the body. She was only recently dumped there and had most likely been stored in a freezer somewhere for several months.

There were an enormous number of potential clues with the body. Forensic investigators found hair on her clothing and pollen from a plum tree, a poplar tree, and a privet bush. In addition, bits of burnt wood were found on her clothes, as if she had been near a burning barrel or bonfire.

The cable ties used to bind her were very specific. They were manufactured exclusively for divisions of the UK postal service – The Royal Mail and Parcelforce.

The duvet cover was typical and could have been purchased at any number of stores throughout the United Kingdom, but the green plastic garbage bags were somewhat unique. They were sold exclusively through the Morrison's grocery store, which had only two locations in the area.

The twine that was wrapped around the duvet was unique as well. Ordinary twine is brown with three twisted strands. This particular twine had four twisted strands and was black. Through some research, investigators determined it to be a distinctive twine often used for rabbit traps.

The duvet and clothes contained dozens of carpet fibers and animal hairs. The carpet fibers had gone through a unique dye process, making them dark red at one end and lighter red at the other. The animal hairs were from a black and tan dog, which was consistent with what the witness had reported from the day Leanne went missing.

One of the most critical pieces of evidence was a dog collar that the killer had used to tighten the plastic bag around her neck. Investigators tracked down 220 wholesalers that carried the particular collar, although anyone could have purchased that collar in any number of local pet shops. However, when they asked a mail-order company called Pets Pajamas for a list of customers who had ordered through the mail, there were only three customers in that area of Leeds. One person, who had purchased six of the same collars, lived within a half mile of Leanne Tiernan – John Taylor.

————

Immediately after announcing the discovery of Leanne's body, police asked the public for help. When Deborah Benjamin heard that the police were looking for anyone that frequented the Lindley Woods to get in touch with the police, she knew she had to call.

Deborah Benjamin told police that she often placed ads in the "lonely hearts" section of the local newspapers. Through those advertisements, she met and dated a man named John Taylor. She explained that he was an avid hunter and often hunted in the same area of Lindley Woods. She had gone there with him on several occasions.

She told detectives that she had eventually ended their relationship because he was obsessed with violent bondage. She explained that he enjoyed tying her hands behind her back with plastic cable ties. One on each wrist, then a third to connect the other two together – precisely the same way

Leanne Tiernan's hands had been bound. Deborah said that Taylor kept the cable ties in a drawer behind his bed and he got them from his work.

Forty-four-year-old John Taylor was known in the area as the "pet man" because he had so many pets. He kept several dogs, ferrets, and owls. He fed the owls baby chicks that he purchased in bulk and kept in large chest freezers.

He was a divorced father of two grown children and lived alone on Cockshott Drive, not far from Houghley Gill. He was generally known as an average man by neighbors, but prior girlfriends and close friends knew of his sadistic tendencies. Although he kept several dogs, he was also known to be particularly cruel to them.

On October 16, 2001, just two months after discovering Leanne's body, police detained and questioned John Taylor.

John Taylor worked for Parcelforce, giving him free access to the same cable ties used to bind Leanne. Twine similar to that used to secure the duvet was found in his house. In his yard were plum trees, poplar trees, and privet bushes, which explained the pollen found on Leanne's body and in her nostrils.

Police searched his home, garage, and backyard for ten days. The first thing they noticed as they walked in the door was a newspaper on his kitchen counter, open to a headline about the discovery of Leanne's body. They found the same type of cable ties, identical dog collars, and three large chest freezers. A tear of green plastic that matched the garbage bags around Leanne's body was found hanging from a nail in his house. His floor, however, was bare. He had pulled up the carpeting recently and burned it in a fire in his backyard. However, investigators found nails that had secured his floorboards and still bore pieces of the red nylon carpet he had removed. The carpet fibers matched the fibers found on Leanne's body. Most importantly, the hairs on Leanne's body matched Taylor's DNA.

Searching his phone records, detectives discovered he had contacted hundreds of women from lonely hearts ads in the newspapers. When police interviewed the women that had dated him, many gave similar stories of his penchant for violent sex and bondage. One woman said he liked to tie her up and lock her in a cupboard. Another said he wanted to tie up her daughter and have sex with her.

Investigators excavated John Taylor's backyard to reveal several graves with the bodies of dogs. One, a black and tan dog that matched the dog hairs found on Leanne's body, had its skull crushed with a meat cleaver.

———

When confronted with the massive amount of evidence against him, Taylor confessed to abducting Leanne. He said he was walking in the opposite direction through Houghley Gill when he saw Leanne Tiernan walking home. As he passed her, he acted impulsively, turned around, and grabbed her from behind. He threw his coat over her head and tied her hands behind her back with a dog leash. He then dragged her back to his nearby home and pushed her onto the bed. When Leanne's mother called and her phone rang, he asked her which buttons to press to turn off the phone.

Taylor explained that Leanne fought to escape but, during the struggle, she fell off the bed and struck her head. He claimed her death was an accident. He had no explanation for why she was found with the cable tie, scarf, and dog collar around her neck other than he used them to move her body more efficiently.

Taylor maintained that her death was an accident until the first day of his trial in February 2002, when he finally admitted murdering her. He pleaded guilty and never explained exactly what happened in his house.

At his sentencing, Judge Justice Astill said:

 "After the death of this girl at your hands, you wanted sexual deviancy with a girl of similar age. That not only demonstrates how dangerous you are but demonstrates your lack of remorse. Not by chance were you in this area for this purpose. You were not acting on impulse. You chose a secluded place and a vulnerable young girl who suited your purposes. This was as cold and calculating as can be imagined. You are a dangerous sexual sadist. Your purpose in kidnapping this young girl was so that you could satisfy your perverted cravings. The suffering you caused her and the suffering you continue to cause those who loved her simply cannot be measured. You must expect to spend the rest of your life in custody."

John Taylor received two life sentences for the crime. After just four months in prison, detectives tested Taylor's DNA against the evidence found in two older rape cases that took place in the same area of Houghley Gill during the late 1980s.

The first happened on October 18, 1988, when a thirty-two-year-old woman walked through Houghley Gill to pick up her children from school. Wearing a mask, Taylor forced her at knifepoint to give him oral sex, then raped her.

The second was on March 1, 1989, when he broke into the home of a twenty-one-year-old woman during the day, tore her clothes off, forced her into the bedroom, and raped her with her small child still in the house. Again, he wore a mask and threatened her with a knife.

Taylor, already facing life in prison, refused to cooperate with police but eventually pleaded guilty when faced with the DNA evidence still on file from the rapes. As a result, he was sentenced to two additional life sentences.

———

John Taylor insisted that was the extent of his crimes but, as detectives continued to dig, they found he was responsible for more and more horrible crimes dating back to 1977. Finally, he was again pulled from prison and confronted with the crimes.

In 1984 he tied a seven-year-old girl to a drainpipe at a church in Bromley, Leeds, and was found guilty of an indecent assault.

He also confessed to another rape of a twenty-seven-year-old woman as she walked with her three children.

In October 2018, Taylor was sentenced to a whole life order, guaranteeing he would never be released from prison.

———

Detectives, however, are certain he is responsible for many more murders. Five murder cases have since been reopened in West Yorkshire and another five in Strathclyde, of Glasgow prostitutes murdered between 1991 and 1997.

In West Yorkshire:

- Twenty-year-old Deborah Alison Wood was found burning near Burley Park Station in Leeds in 1996. She had been frozen for some time and was found wrapped in bedding and plastic trash bags.

- The body of thirty-eight-year-old Yvonne Fitt was found in Lindley Woods in January 1992, just feet from where Leanne's body was found.

- Thirteen-year-old Lindsay Rimer was found strangled at the bottom of a canal five months after her disappearance.

- Nineteen-year-old Rebecca Hall was found dead in an alley just thirteen days after her disappearance in April 2001.

Strathclyde police have reopened the murder investigations of Diane McInally (23), Karen McGregor (26), Leona McGovern (22), Marjorie Roberts (34), and Tracey Wylde (21), all of whom were Glasgow prostitutes that were murdered between 1991 and 1997.

CHAPTER 2
THE CLOSET

The streets of Akron, Ohio, were bare in the pre-dawn hours of May 2, 2003. When a caller reported three young boys drinking from their garden hose at 3:00 a.m., police thought nothing of it. But when another caller reported three boys in the same area rummaging through garbage cans and dumpsters, police decided to send out a patrol car to track down the kids.

The Akron patrol officers who were making their usual rounds throughout the neighborhood of Kenmore, on the southwest edge of the city, were the ones who got the call. They pointed their spotlight on a residential sidewalk and saw something strange. Three young boys were wandering aimlessly down the sidewalk. They were shoeless and wearing almost no clothes other than worn-out pajamas, shorts, and t-shirts. All three were beyond thin. Their cheeks were sunken and their arms were little more than skin draped over bones. The youngest had a towel wrapped around his tiny ankle, while the oldest boy had bloodied fingers.

The boys seemed confused and afraid to speak to the officers. They acted like the uniformed men were from another planet – as if this was their first experience in the outside world that we all take for granted. But, unfortunately, the real story wasn't that far from the truth.

Initially, the officers could get little more than the boys' names and ages out of them: Daryl – fourteen, Tyler – ten, and Jesse – eight. They could tell, however, that the boys were hungry. So, the officers put them in the back of their squad car, drove them to an all-night sandwich shop, and bought them foot-long sub sandwiches and Gatorade. The young boys demolished the subs and guzzled the Gatorade like wild animals devouring a kill. They had never eaten anything so delicious. Moreover, the meal helped the boys develop a sense of trust in the two officers.

With a full belly, the three boys were much more talkative and explained that they had never had food like that in their lives. They'd heard of it but had never really tasted it. The police officers gazed in disbelief. How was that even possible? Then the boys explained what their lives had been like up until that point.

The story the three boys told seemed a little far-fetched. The two officers weren't sure if they could believe it. After the officers heard their story, they packed them back into the squad car and drove back to their home on Florida Avenue. As the car pulled up to the curb in front of the grayish-blue two-story house, the three boys screamed, "No, you can't take us back there!" They were panicked and thought the officers didn't believe them. However, the officers reassured them that they wouldn't make them go back into the house.

The boys sat in the car with the officers until another squad car pulled up behind them. Then another. And another. Blue and red lights flickered in every direction. Then a team of officers approached the front door and the boys watched their mother argue with them before the team entered the house.

Fifteen minutes later, the boys' mother, Mary Rowles, and her girlfriend, Alice Jenkins, were brought out in handcuffs and put in a squad car. Then three more children, the boys' siblings, were escorted from the home and emergency crews took all six children to the hospital.

———

Mary Rowles had considered herself a victim as far back as her friends could remember. To her, life was something that happened to her – she never had a choice. She felt it so assuredly that she tattooed the phrase "Victim of Life" on her forearm in her late teens. Everything that happened in her life, she believed, was the fault of someone else. She took responsibility for nothing.

Mary dropped out of high school halfway through her junior year at age sixteen, when she found herself pregnant. Immediately after giving birth to her son, Daryl, she was pregnant again with another boy, Danny. She worked for a brief time at a Burger King and married the father of the two boys, but neither the job nor the marriage lasted very long. From that point on, she lived off of public assistance.

Over the next six years, Mary Rowles gave birth to four more children. At just twenty-four years old, she was an unemployed, single mother of six children from five different men.

A close friend later recalled that Mary Rowles loved babies – but she didn't necessarily like children. She was essentially a child herself, or at least acted like one. For Mary, each of her children was just a meal ticket that got her more and more government assistance.

Just before she gave birth to her sixth child, Mary had had enough of men and began to frequent local lesbian clubs. It was in the mid-1990s that she met Alice Jenkins at the Roseto Club in southeast Akron. The windowless dive bar catered almost exclusively to lesbian clientele and was known for its "drag king" nights, where female performers dressed in masculine drag – a flip on the well-known drag queen nights held at many gay bars.

Twenty-one-year-old Alice "Jamie" Jenkins had been openly gay since she was fifteen. She stood at just four feet eleven inches and weighed only ninety pounds, but her short-cropped hair matched her headstrong, aggressive demeanor. Having grown up with three brothers, Alice was tougher than most boys her age despite her petite frame. She also knew her way around cars better than most men and had worked in a car parts store since she was fifteen.

The oldest of Mary's six children was only eight when Alice moved in. Until then, life for the children had already been less than ideal, since Mary barely acknowledged their existence. When Alice moved in, however, their situation went from bad to worse. Exponentially worse.

———

Shortly after Alice's arrival, the two oldest boys, Daryl and Danny, moved in with their father. Then Marissa moved in with her father as well. Mary shared custody of these three children, which required that they spend their weekends with her and Alice, but the remaining three children lived with Mary full-time.

As far as Alice Jenkins was concerned, Mary had been doing a horrible job as a mother. She believed she could do better – through extreme discipline.

Ever since she was a little girl, Alice needed to be the center of attention in every aspect of her life. What little attention Mary *did* give to her children, Alice wanted directed at herself. In her opinion, the children deserved nothing. Especially the boys.

Immediately upon moving in with the family, Alice took authoritative control. From that point forward, the children were to address her as "Daddy" or "ma'am."

For the first three years of their relationship, Mary and Alice shared a home with another lesbian couple – Mary's sister and her partner, Karen. During those early years, Karen noticed a pattern developing. Although five boys lived in the house, she rarely saw most of them except for the infant, Caleb. They were usually confined to their bedroom or in "time-out," sitting on their hands in the stairwell and not allowed to speak. Mary's daughter Marissa, however, was allowed to live an everyday life amongst the other women of the house.

The boys shared two bedrooms upstairs. Alice and Mary had sparsely equipped each room with little besides a mattress on the floor. Although there was a neighborhood playground near their home, the boys were never allowed to go. That would have meant an adult had to watch over them and neither Alice nor Mary wanted any part of that. Although Karen didn't see any physical abuse during those first three years, she knew the situation wasn't on a good path.

———

By 1999 Karen and Mary's sister had moved out of the home, leaving the children alone with Mary and Alice. Mary, diagnosed with multiple sclerosis, spent much of her time in a stupor from morphine and medical marijuana that she had been prescribed. She paid little to no attention to the children at all, leaving Alice in complete control.

During the week, while Danny and Daryl were with their father, Tyler and Jesse were confined to their bedroom. Every day, before Alice went to work, she tied the boys' wrists and ankles to their beds. Then, when she arrived home from work, she untied them and brought them downstairs for dinner, which usually consisted of macaroni and cheese or a hot dog. They returned to their bedroom immediately after finishing their meal.

Over time the boys, both less than six years old, figured out how to untie themselves during the day. They went downstairs and watched television with their mother and Caleb, but they had to return to their room when Alice came home.

Frustrated that the boys were able to escape, Alice separated them. Jesse went into one room, Tyler into another. Alice tied the two opposing bedroom doors together with a rope in the hallway outside, making it impossible for them to escape. Every day, from 8:00 a.m. until 4:00 p.m., they were alone in their rooms: void of toys and unable to speak to each other.

Their only form of communication was to tap out musical beats on the wall that separated them. They could see each other for an hour downstairs at dinner in the evenings, but afterward it was back to the bedroom.

With no access to a bathroom from either bedroom, dinner and breakfast were their only opportunities to relieve themselves. If they missed that chance, the boys had learned to pull up the carpet in the corner of their bedrooms, urinate beneath it, and then replace it.

During their meals downstairs, their mother rarely said a word to the young boys. They had begun to assume that how they were being treated was normal. That was the way life was.

Then one day, something changed. Alice had decided that Jesse and Tyler deserved no time downstairs at all. So, instead of seeing their mother and Caleb downstairs, they were given a meal in their room. Each received dry cereal in the morning and half a peanut butter sandwich in the evening. Alice stood over them while they took a few minutes to eat. Then she locked the doors again. Water or anything to drink at all was a rarity, as Alice knew that would lead to them having to go to the bathroom.

Jesse and Tyler were fed at different times and weren't allowed to see each other at all. For almost a year, the two brothers hadn't seen each other, their mother, or their other siblings. Only Alice.

————

Marissa opened the doors to Jesse and Tyler's bedrooms one morning, fed them, and got them dressed. It was their first day of school. Unfortunately, the two boys barely even understood the concept of school. They couldn't read or write, couldn't tie their shoes, and barely even knew how to use a toilet.

During their brief time at school, none of the faculty said a word about their lack of proper clothing, malnourished bodies, or odd mannerisms. However, it ended as quickly as it started. Within three weeks, Alice and Mary pulled them out of school; from then on, the school district listed them as homeschooled children.

———

In 2000, Mary regained full custody of the two older brothers, Daryl and Danny. They shared one of the upstairs bedrooms while Tyler and Jesse shared another, almost always locked inside.

One afternoon, Tyler and Jesse looked out their second-story bedroom window and noticed other children on the sidewalk below. The boys opened the window and said hello. Although they had never met them before, for just a few minutes the two boys had friends. The kids below asked them to come down and play, but before they even had a chance to answer, Alice burst into the room and slammed the window shut. She screamed at them and told them they knew better than to open the window. Then she grabbed them both by the wrist, opened the small closet in the room, and threw them inside. The boys listened as she pushed a heavy wooden dresser in front of the door and left the room.

Jesse and Tyler spent the next several days in the closet, then eventually Alice installed a padlock outside the door. Inside was nothing but walls. Three feet by five feet. No shelving or bar on which to hang clothes and only a sliver of light that peeked in from beneath the door. The closet became their home for the next three years.

Alice no longer scheduled meals for the boys. Instead, they got fed when Alice decided to provide for them. When they did eat, it was always dry cereal for breakfast and half a peanut butter sandwich for dinner. They tried their best to make it last and eat as slowly as possible, but Alice didn't want to put up with that. She gave them only two minutes.

They also had limited time to use the bathroom. If they accidentally splashed on the rim of the toilet, they were forced to lick it clean. Inevitably, they often slept in their own urine.

When Alice and Mary left the house, they put Marissa in charge of watching over her brothers. The boys begged Marissa to let them out of the closet. One day she let them out and when they all ran downstairs to get something to eat, they were astounded to find that the cabinets and fridge were overflowing with food. There was plenty of food in the house to feed them all; Alice was withholding it from them. The boys gorged themselves on as much food as they could in the short time they had, but Alice was furious when she found out what they had done. That was the first time she forced them to eat feces.

On three occasions, when they had done something wrong – such as talking too loudly in the closet or taking too long to eat – Alice punished them by forcing them to eat a bowl of dog feces. Then, when they threw it up, she forced them to eat it again.

The boys learned that the "throw-up thing," as they called it, could come in handy. For example, when they had a peanut butter sandwich, they learned to throw it up and eat it again, making them feel like they got more food.

———

Tyler received the most physical abuse from Alice. His father was African-American and she regularly screamed racial slurs at him. Alice pushed him down the stairs once, hit his toes with a hammer, burned him with cigarettes, regularly beat him with a belt while making sure to hit his genitals, and kicked him in the groin with her steel-toed work boots.

Alice punished the boys for reading books without permission, using too much toothpaste, or speaking too loudly in their rooms. All the while, their mother sat downstairs and had almost forgotten they even existed.

———

Marissa was only nine years old, but she knew something was terribly wrong with the situation at her mother's house. Her five brothers were treated horribly, locked in rooms, and rarely fed. When she returned to her father's home every week, she told him and her stepmother what was happening. She explained to her father that the boys were locked in their bedrooms that reeked of urine and feces.

In 1999 and 2000, Marissa's father and stepmother, Brady and Lisa Postlethwaite, called Summit County Children Services Board more than 100 times.

Children Services, however, only came to the house on two occasions. Both times Alice and Mary were warned ahead of time. The children were bathed and brought to the living room to prepare for the visit. Alice poured a garbage bag full of toys onto the floor – toys the boys had never seen before. While the children played with the toys, Alice and Mary spoke to CSB representatives. During the visits they didn't talk to the emaciated children, didn't go upstairs, and never asked to see their bedrooms. They only saw that the living room was tidy, spoke briefly to Mary and Alice, and left.

Immediately after they left, the toys went back into the garbage bag and the boys were locked back into their rooms.

Regardless, the Postlethwaites continued to call CSB. On one occasion, when Lisa Postlethwaite went to the house to pick up Marissa at the end of the weekend, she witnessed a child's car carrier upside down and facing the corner of the living room. One of the boys, most likely Caleb, was strapped into the car seat and hanging upside down. It was a form of punishment that Marissa had mentioned in the past. Marissa told her father and stepmother that Alice had kept the boy upside down in the car carrier for so long that he had no choice but to urinate on himself.

However, the regular calls to SCCS eventually backfired on the Postlethwaites. They were threatened with prosecution if they continued to file unsubstantiated allegations against Mary Rowles.

Mary and Alice, in turn, took the opportunity to allege that the Postlethwaithes were abusing Marissa and their own children. As a result, Mary sued for full custody of Marissa. Sadly, by 2002 Brady and Lisa Postlethwaithe were forced to surrender custody of Marissa or risk losing their other children as well. As a result, all six children were now under Alice and Mary's control full-time.

Although Marissa was allowed to sleep in a real bed, eat regular meals, and had full access to the house, Alice put her to work. She put Marissa in charge of feeding her siblings, taking them to the bathroom, and ensuring they stayed in line – but only when Alice said so.

But all was not well between Alice and Mary. Their relationship had deteriorated. In April 2000, Mary gathered all six shoeless children and they left home on foot, running frantically toward a friend's house several blocks away. Alice pursued them in her car and gunned the gas pedal when she saw them. She hopped the curb, trying to run them over as they ran down the sidewalk.

When Mary and her children arrived at the friend's home, she told her of the horrible abuse that Alice had subjected the children to and that she had kicked Tyler down the stairs. The friend called Child Services but, again, they did nothing. Mary inevitably went back home. Several days after the incident, Alice called the friend and threatened to kill her if she didn't mind her own business.

There were still more calls to Child Services. In 2002, Alice called a plumber, Daniel Odum, to the home to fix a sink in the downstairs bathroom. With his head under the sink, he heard a loud thud coming from the living room and then a child crying. Odum stopped what he was doing and peeked his head around the corner of the living room to find Alice with her hands on the shoulders of a small child, shaking him violently. Startled, he turned back into the bathroom and finished his work. When he had fixed the sink, he walked back into the living room to find five young boys sitting with their legs crossed in front of them, silent and not moving.

When Odum got home and told his wife of the way Alice was shaking the child, they called the Children Services Board. They reported the incident but never heard anything about it after that.

By early 2003 the children were only being fed once a week and they hadn't seen their mother in months. They knew they had to do something to escape. Danny and Daryl managed to get outside once, ran down the street to a gas station, and tried to call their father, whom they hadn't spoken to in years. Before they got a chance to make the call, however, police picked them up. Mary and Alice had reported them as runaways.

They were taken to a juvenile detention center but were too afraid to tell authorities what their conditions were like at home and were returned to Mary and Alice.

In early May, Jesse and Daryl were locked in the closet as usual when the door opened. All of their siblings stood in the room except for Danny – he was still locked in the bedroom across the hall. Finally, Marissa explained that Alice and Mary were asleep and they needed to leave. It was now or never.

Using his fingertips, Daryl removed the nails holding the upstairs window shut. Daryl, Jesse, and Tyler then crawled out of the window and onto the roof that hung over the front porch. Trying to be as quiet as possible, Daryl put Jesse – who, at eight years old, weighed only twenty-eight pounds – on his shoulders, carefully held on to the gutter, and climbed over the edge of the roof line. But the gutter wasn't strong enough and snapped, creating a loud crash as the boys fell to the ground.

The children were frozen and silent for several seconds, watching Mary and Alice's bedroom to see if the light had turned on. It didn't. Tyler still needed to get off the roof, but no gutter was left. After a few minutes of silent coaxing, Tyler finally jumped but sprained his ankle when he hit the ground. Jesse and Daryl got Tyler to his feet and helped him hobble down the sidewalk.

The three boys wandered the streets of the Kenmore neighborhood, looking for help but having no idea where to turn. They drank water from a neighbor's garden hose and rummaged through trash cans looking for something to put around Tyler's ankle, or perhaps some discarded food. Police found them moments later.

Emergency crews took the children to the hospital, some staying for more than six weeks. Their bodies had been so malnourished that they had stopped growing.

Mary Rowles and Alice Jenkins were both charged with five felony counts of child endangering plus an extra two counts of felonious assault for Alice. Both women were released on $1,000 bail each. Eventually, the charges grew to a fifty-five count indictment, including the psychological abuse of Marissa.

Initially, both women pleaded not guilty to most of the crimes but later pleaded guilty. In January 2004, both were sentenced to thirty years in prison.

————

The dormitory-style living conditions of Alice and Mary's prison cells were far better than the lives they provided for the six children. In 2018 both women requested an early release from prison, claiming that prison had changed them. Both requests were denied.

————

The abuse had a lasting effect on the children. Malnourishment caused two of the boys to lose much of their eyesight. In addition, many of them suffered post-traumatic stress disorder, alcoholism, and drug abuse in their teenage and adult years. Jesse's abuse created a condition called trichotillomania, which causes him to pull out his eyelashes when stressed.

After spending time in foster care, Caleb and Jesse were adopted by a family in Scottsdale, Arizona, who had fostered forty children throughout the years. Caleb, however, spent eighteen months in a treatment facility for troubled youth. He was diagnosed with severe reactive attachment disorder, had legal trouble, and was placed on probation.

Danny, who shared a father with Daryl, lived with his father. He had trouble with drugs and alcohol for a time and eventually moved in with his grandmother.

Daryl opted for foster care rather than to live with his father. At nineteen he sued Summit County Children Services for $25,000. The lawsuit stated that during each of these home visits, there was open, obvious, and overwhelming evidence of ongoing abuse and neglect of himself and his siblings. It's unclear, however, if anything ever became of the lawsuit.

Marissa went to live with her father and stepmother. At eighteen she gave birth and later married a man with three children of his own. Three weeks after their wedding, she dropped her children off at daycare and was driving her minivan home when a man in a Jaguar crossed the yellow line while going ninety miles per hour, racing another car. Twenty-six-year-old Marissa and the man driving the Jaguar were killed on impact.

The siblings lost contact with Tyler, who tattooed Marissa's birthday, the date of her death, and a heart on his forehead.

CHAPTER 3
THE CHRISTMAS TREE FARM MURDERS

Ed and Minnie Maurin were in their late fifties when they married in 1961 in southwest Washington state. Although their love affair started later in life, it was destined to last. Minnie had four children from her previous marriage to a farmer who had died in the 1950s. By 1985, eighty-three-year-old Minnie and eighty-one-year-old Ed had fourteen grandchildren and fourteen great-grand-children.

The couple was very active in the tiny township of Ethel, Washington, but to call Ethel tiny was being generous. There wasn't actually a town – it was more a junction of two lonely, rural highways with a small market and gas station. The nearest city was Chehalis, Washington, twenty miles to the north.

Minnie and Ed were active in the surrounding communities. They owned a 120-acre farm that they leased out to grow Christmas trees and the couple was known for hosting a Christmas luncheon every year at their farmhouse, to which they invited members of their local Catholic Church and community.

Friends were scheduled to help set up the house for the party at 10:30 on the morning of December 19, 1985 but, when they arrived, the doors of their home were locked and the blinds were closed. The Maurins had always made a point to leave their blinds open, especially during the holiday season, when their Christmas tree was decorated with lights that shone through the window. It was very out of the ordinary.

The Maurin family car was gone. Perhaps they had forgotten about the party. It was unlikely, but it happens with age. But when her daughter, Hazel, showed up at noon, she knew that wasn't the case. She had just spoken about it at length with her mother in the late afternoon of the day before.

After trying every possible point of entry, family members went to the back of the house, broke a window, and opened the back door.

Once inside, they found no sign of Ed and Minnie. The only thing that seemed out of place was a shoebox on the bathroom floor. The box had been opened and bank statements were spread all over the floor.

The family members called relatives, friends, and church members to be on the lookout for Ed and Minnie Maurin. However, by 6:30 that evening they were nowhere to be found and it was time to alert the Lewis County Sheriff.

———

When detectives arrived, they noticed another thing in the house that seemed out of place. Minnie's purse had been tucked behind the couch with a newspaper covering it. It looked as if she had tried to hide it. Knowing that she would have never left the house without her purse, officers knew something was wrong.

Throughout the night, police, relatives, and friends searched for the elderly couple. They checked local hospitals and drove the extensive backroads that weaved through the area, looking for their green 1969 Chrysler Newport, but they found nothing.

The next day, December 20, police put out an all-points bulletin to be on the lookout for their green Chrysler and alerted the public to help search for the car too. By noon someone had found the vehicle.

Several people had reported seeing the car parked in the northeast corner of the largest shopping center in town, Yard Birds. When police arrived, the car's windows were covered with frost, blocking the view to the inside. But when they opened the car door, they found a gruesome crime scene.

The entire front interior of the car was covered with blood spatter. Blood dripped from the dashboard, down the door panels, and soaked the front seat. Although there were no bodies in the car, it was a safe bet that whoever's blood it was, was now dead.

The dashboard was peppered with small holes and tiny pellets were embedded in the console. More pellets littered the floorboards. It was clearly buckshot from a shotgun. Someone had been shot at close range inside the car. Covering the driver's side seat was a large red blanket. A man's hat and a woman's tennis shoe lay on the floor.

———

Detectives spoke to employees of Yard Birds to see if anyone had seen who parked the car in the lot. Luckily, several witnesses had seen a man walking away from the vehicle. Employees were on their lunch break the previous day and saw a man, aged twenty to thirty, leaving the car. He had brown hair that was not quite shoulder-length and four to five days of stubble on his face. He wore blue jeans, logging boots, and a green army jacket. The man also appeared to be concealing a rifle wrapped in a towel or blanket.

Although the description was thorough, it could have described hundreds of men in the Lewis County area in the 1980s. Regardless, police sketch artists created a composite drawing of the suspect and released it to the public.

———

Five days had passed and there was no sign of the elderly couple. Then, on December 24, Christmas Eve, a man was driving on Stearns Hill Road – a secluded, gravel logging road ten miles west of Chehalis – when he saw what he thought was a department store mannequin in the ditch on the side of the road. When he got out of his truck for a closer look, however, he quickly realized it was a woman's body and called the police.

When investigators arrived, they found the body of an older woman who had died a very violent death: a shotgun blast to the back of her head. They followed bloody drag marks near her body further down the gravel road into the bushes about thirty feet away. There they found a plastic comb, men's glasses, and the upper half of a pair of false teeth. When they continued further into the bushes, they found the body of an elderly male. He, too, had been shot in the back of the head and neck with a shotgun. It was obvious that the victims were Ed and Minnie Maurin.

Detectives found an essential clue in Ed's front pants pocket: a withdrawal receipt from Lewis Family Savings.

When detectives spoke to employees at Lewis Family Savings, they learned that early in the morning on December 19, Ed Maurin called and asked them to prepare $8,500 in cash. Ed explained that he wanted to help one of his children buy a new car and needed cash.

Shortly before 11:00 a.m., Ed walked into the bank alone and asked for the withdrawal. When the teller suggested he get the money as a cashier's check, he declined, stating that he needed to have it in cash – all $100 bills.

When detectives spoke to family members, however, none said they were planning on buying a car. Investigators now believed that the killer had been waiting in the car with Minnie Maurin while Ed went into the bank to make the withdrawal. Shortly after stealing their money, the killer had them drive to Stearns Hill Road where they shot them both, then drove their car to Yard Birds.

————

When the news of Ed and Minnie's horrific death spread through the rural communities of Lewis County, the people were terrified. The small towns where families had typically left their doors unlocked became cautious of every stranger they met. Christmas would never be the same for the family and friends of Ed and Minnie Maurin.

————

The composite drawing circulating through the media was bringing in lots of leads; every one of them had to be scrutinized.

Police continued their investigations and analyzed Ed and Minnie's car and farmhouse more closely. Unfortunately, the only fingerprints found inside the vehicle or house were from Ed, Minnie, or their family. As with any case like this, police began their investigation by questioning the extended family.

One family member stuck out to detectives more than the rest – Minnie's grandson, Mike Hadaller. Mike was in his late teens, was a heavy drinker, and was rumored to be involved with drugs. In addition, he had a juvenile record, having once broken into his own father's safe to steal money.

Police interviewed the boy, who unequivocally denied involvement in his grandparents' murder. Mike worked for his father's logging company and said that, at 5:00 a.m. that morning, he and his father were on their way to work. They arrived at work at 5:30, where he worked the entire day. His work foreman later corroborated his alibi. Ultimately, he was given a polygraph test which he passed. He was eliminated as a suspect.

One by one, other family members were eliminated as suspects, as were the Christmas tree farm employees. The fact was, the elderly couple had no enemies whatsoever. Police were stumped as to who might have committed such a heinous act.

Several other witnesses came forward to report they had seen the Maurins' car on the morning of December 19. Lucy Shriver and her seventeen-year-old son, Jason, reported seeing the green car as they drove to the dentist that morning. They had noticed two men in the car with Ed and Minnie.

Another witness reported seeing the car at 10:45 that morning with one man in the back. Yet another claimed to have seen one man driving the car at 11:30 that morning. Another female witness told police she saw the car empty, parked alongside the road near where the bodies were later found. Still another witness in the same area claimed to have seen the car going toward the site of the murder with three people in it, then later rushing away with only one person.

Another witness claimed to have seen a white van parked in front of the Maurins' home in the early morning hours of December 19.

Although the eyewitness reports and the time that Ed had withdrawn the money gave detectives a more accurate time-line of events, they were still no closer to having a suspect.

———

Seven years had passed with no solid leads in the case, but detectives kept looking through all the old tips, interviewing and re-interviewing witnesses.

One of the old leads that hadn't been thoroughly investigated was that of a man named Leslie George. George told police that he used to hang out and do drugs with two brothers who were originally from Mossyrock, in eastern Lewis County, and had a reputation for mayhem. They had recently moved to the Chehalis area at the time of the murders and were known to deal drugs. He claimed they usually robbed people to get the money to buy the drugs.

Their names were Ricky and John Riffe and George told detectives that he'd overheard them planning a robbery just a week before the murder. George said he had once mentioned Ed and Minnie Maurin to the brothers. As they drove past the Maurin farmhouse one night, George pointed toward the house and said,

 "If you're looking for someone with money, these people are loaded."

George said he had also given Ricky Riffe a shotgun that he wanted to have sawed off. George was a long-haul trucker and wanted the shotgun to keep in his truck for protection. He claimed that he gave Riffe the shotgun a week or so before the killings, but when he repeatedly asked for it back, Riffe didn't return it. Months later, Riffe finally returned the shotgun but George said he had a bad feeling about it. He had a suspicion that the gun had been used in the killing.

George hid the gun at his father's home for a few weeks until his father had the same uneasiness about the weapon and threw it into Lake Mayfield. Detectives sent dive teams to scour the lake but never located the shotgun.

George told detectives that they should talk to Ricky Riffe's ex-wife, Robin Riffe.

When detectives tried to locate Robin Riffe, they realized she was in an Arizona prison on a drug conviction. Working with the Arizona Department of Corrections, they interviewed Robin by telephone. When they explained that they were investigating a double homicide case in Lewis county, she immediately blurted out, "You mean the two old people?"

Robin Riffe knew precisely what case they were referring to. She said that she dropped Ricky and John Riffe off at a store about a mile from the Maurin farmhouse on the night of December 18. Her husband told her to pick them up a few hours later, but they weren't there when she returned. The next day she got a call to meet them on Stearns Hill Road. She said she saw a body lying in the ditch and Ricky told his brother to take her back home.

————

Detectives had their first real witness but Robin was far from reliable. She had a long history of criminal offenses and there was no way the prosecution was going to trial with only her testimony to back them up. They needed more evidence.

After her release from prison, detectives kept close tabs on Robin Riffe. They knew there would come a time when they would need her to testify. Every six months or so, they called to ask if she had heard anything about her ex-husband, but in 1995 she suddenly died after having a heart valve replaced. They were back to square one and the case went cold for another fourteen years.

————

Nineteen years after the murders, in 2004, Lewis County Sheriff's office brought in new investigators to look into cold cases. Detective Bruce Kimsey was tasked with digging through old evidence and looking at hundreds of tips with a fresh set of eyes.

Kimsey discovered that Ricky and John Riffe had left the area years earlier and moved to King Salmon, Alaska. In cooperation with local police, Kimsey traveled to Alaska to interview the brothers.

Questioning the brothers, however, was useless. Ricky refused to answer questions and John claimed he couldn't remember what had happened twenty-four years earlier. Although they both failed polygraph tests, prosecutors were still no closer to bringing them to trial.

Kimsey then spoke to Robin Riffe's sister, Tammy Graham, who talked about Christmas back in 1985. Rick and Robin were both unemployed and had three children, but when they showed up at Tammy's home Christmas morning, the entire family came dressed in new clothes and bearing gifts for the whole family. Rick also had a large amount of cocaine with him. It was clear that Ricky had somehow acquired a large amount of money just before Christmas.

Tammy also recalled that Rick had randomly asked her husband if shotgun pellets were traceable.

While re-interviewing witnesses who had seen the Maurins in their car that fateful morning, Kimsey spoke to Jason Shriver again. Shriver was just seventeen when he saw Ed, Minnie, and the two men in the green Chrysler that morning, but the image was ingrained in his mind forever. He would never forget it. A lot of time had passed since he saw them and he was now ready to talk.

Jason Shriver admitted to detectives that he knew who Ricky and John Riffe were when he saw them in the car with the Maurins. He knew them by reputation and they scared him to death. He told detectives that, on that morning as he and his mother drove to the dentist, he recognized John Riffe in the back passenger side seat sitting directly behind his brother, who was in the front passenger side. Minnie sat next to John and Ed was driving the car.

As they passed the car, Jason saw John and waved at him. John nodded in return and both cars went their own way. But after the murders, John and Ricky Riffe confronted him. They told the boy that if he ever told a soul that he recognized them in the car that day, they would kill him and then kill his mother.

Years had passed; Jason was now forty-one years old and his mother had passed away. He was no longer worried about retaliation and told police that he would testify against the Riffe brothers.

————

On July 8, 2012, Alaska state troopers served a warrant for the arrest of Ricky Riffe. John Gregory Riffe had died of natural causes just a week before the arrest warrant was served.

When Detective Kimsey and Alaska state troopers entered the home, a gravelly voice from a back room shouted, "Who the fuck are you?" Ricky Riffe was no longer the young man he was when he murdered the Maurins. He was on oxygen, his skin was weathered, and he had long and scraggly gray hair.

When Kimsey told him he was under arrest for the 1985 murders, he only said, "Well, I better get my medications."

Ricky Riffe was charged with two counts of first-degree murder, two counts of first-degree kidnapping, one count of robbery in the first degree, and one count of burglary in the first degree.

Dozens of witnesses testified against him, including Leslie George's wife, Deborah, who he had been having an online affair with for the past year through Facebook.

During their online relationship, Riffe told Deborah details about the crime that law enforcement hadn't released. She said that Riffe told her that he had hit Ed in the head before he shot him because Ed refused to get out of the car.

During the trial, Deborah George also told the jury about Riffe's strange sexual requests. He told her he wanted to have sex with her where he had killed Ed and Minnie. He also told her he wanted her to have sex with a dog and a donkey.

The bestiality remarks weren't the first time Riffe had requested that of a woman. Robin Riffe told detectives that, years earlier, he had asked her the same thing. In a separate case, Riffe was charged with sexually abusing the ten-year-old daughter of a woman he had lived with during the 1980s.

Ricky Riffe was found guilty of all charges and sentenced to 103 years in prison. In 2014 he was given another six years and three months for the sexual abuse of a child charge.

CHAPTER 4
A PERFECT HOLIDAY

Although her parents were divorced, seven-year-old Sarah Smith had lived a happy, normal life with her younger brother Chris and a mother who cared for her. But that happy, normal life came crashing to pieces in October 1992 when her mother, Lianne Smith, began dating Martin Smith.

When Lianne and Martin Smith met through a local dating agency in North Tyneside, UK, they must have considered it ironic that they shared the same last name. Lianne was going through a divorce and the two hit it off quickly. Within months, Martin Smith had moved in with Lianne and her two children from her previous marriage in their small camping trailer.

Martin Smith considered himself a psychic and hypnotist, despite having no abilities in the field. He had once had a very small part on a single episode of a television show called Britain's Most Haunted but, in reality, he was nothing more than a failed stage performer.

Martin was also a controlling, manipulative narcissist who lacked the slightest bit of empathy for others. From the beginning of their relationship, he worked to amplify Lianne's already dependent personality.

Within months of moving in together, Lianne had become entirely dependent upon him and unable to make even simple decisions about their life. She needed to be told what to do in every aspect of her day-to-day life, from what to wear to what job to take and even what food to eat. She had completely lost control and was emotionally and psychologically dependent upon Martin.

Worse yet, Lianne lost control of her ability to protect her children. Martin began beating her son, Chris, and sexually abusing her daughter, Sarah. Lianne knew what was happening but chose to turn a blind eye, not wanting to lose the only thing she cared about in her life: Martin.

Martin would regularly go into Sarah's bedroom and tell her that he would hypnotize her. But, of course, Sarah knew the subtext of what that really meant. Knowing he would do what he wanted with her no matter what she did, Sarah pretended to be under his spell while he raped her. Afterward, he would count down to one, snap his fingers, and tell her to wake up. When he asked how she felt, not wanting to cause trouble, the young girl would reply that she had a nice dream.

Unbelievably, Lianne took a job with the Children's Social Services Welfare Department. While trying to help other people's children, her own children were beaten and molested by her partner at home.

Within a year, Martin had refused to let Lianne and the children visit with their relatives. As a result, Chris and Sarah were completely cut-off from their grandparents.

Lianne's job with Social Services didn't last long. Martin refused to seek work as anything other than a psychic, which inevitably meant he didn't work at all. The family had no money and he forced Lianne to turn to prostitution for the family to survive.

Martin advertised that Lianne would perform "holistic services" for men. He would drive her to appointments and wait in the car while she had sex with these random men.

Constantly struggling for money, the family moved around regularly and the children were taken out of school to be homeschooled. Eventually, the schools and social services lost track of the two children.

The family eventually moved south to Staffordshire, England, and in July 2004, Lianne gave birth to her third child, Becky. A few years afterward, Sarah escaped the abuse when she left for college. Chris, too, escaped when he was kicked out of the house not long after.

While away at college, Sarah couldn't help but worry about her baby sister, Becky. She knew that Becky was now alone with an abusive pedophile and reported her years of abuse to the police.

On November 1, 2007, Martin Smith was arrested for the rape and abuse of Sarah Smith. Unbelievably, the now-known pedophile was released on bail back to a home with a three-year-old baby girl. Two days later, he, Lianne, and Becky disappeared.

———

Martin and Lianne Smith often moved throughout Spain, near Barcelona, for the next two and a half years. Knowing a European warrant was out for his arrest, they kept a low profile and used fake names.

Again, Martin refused to work. Lianne worked as an English teacher for a time and again worked as a prostitute.

In June 2009, Lianne gave birth to a boy, Daniel. For a time, Lianne was making enough money for the family of four to settle down. Daniel was put into daycare and five-year-old Becky attended preschool.

In 2010 their home was broken into and Martin Smith called the police. However, Martin and Lianne had let down their guard; they didn't think that police would want to see their identification. When they couldn't produce accurate identification, police began looking less at the break-in and more into them. It didn't take long for Spanish police to realize that he was Martin Smith and wanted on a European arrest warrant.

Martin Smith was quickly arrested and extradited back to the United Kingdom to face the charges of sexual abuse and rape of a child.

Lianne was at a loss. Without Martin to tell her what to do, she became frantic. She had relied on him for so long to make every decision in her life. Forced to make decisions for herself, Lianne was obsessed with the fear that her children would be taken away. Authorities knew she was well aware of Martin's abuse and allowed it to go on for years. For the next week, her brain stewed in Spain while Martin sat in jail.

Eight days after Martin's arrest, Lianne gathered her children together and asked them a serious question: "Would you rather live a few great days with me or a long time without me?" Eleven-month-old Daniel, of course, could barely comprehend what she was saying, let alone reply with a meaningful answer. Five-year-old Becky told her mother that she wanted to stay with her, of course.

On May 15, 2010, Lianne Smith packed a small suitcase and the three of them traveled an hour north of Barcelona to the popular seaside tourist town of Lloret de Mar, where she checked them into room 101 at the Miramar Hotel. She told the children it would be "the perfect holiday."

For two days, Lianne played with Becky and Daniel and took photos of them eating ice cream on the sandy beaches surrounding the crystal-clear aqua-blue water.

On the evening of May 17, Lianne put the kids to bed at 7:00 p.m. and spent the next hour sitting on the bed, watching them sleep. Once they were asleep, she took a plastic shopping bag, wrapped it around Daniel's head, and held it over his face until he stopped breathing. Moments later, she did the same to Becky, holding her legs down with her own legs to keep her from getting free.

That night, Lianne slept in the same bed with her children and snuggled their cold bodies. The entire next day, Lianne didn't leave her hotel room. She and Martin had agreed on a suicide pact. If anything happened that would separate them, they had both agreed to kill themselves.

She wrote a series of notes. One, written to her dead children, read,

 "I love you very much. I wanted to give you a lovely life together. I'm very sorry."

Locked inside the hotel room, she tried desperately to kill herself. She attempted to hang herself, slit her wrists, suffocate, and drown herself. But, no matter how hard she tried, she couldn't pull it off.

The next afternoon at 1:30, she walked down to the Miramar Hotel front desk and asked the receptionist,

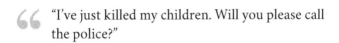

"I've just killed my children. Will you please call the police?"

When police arrived, it seemed like Lianne Smith was on another planet. They took her into an adjacent hotel room while forensic teams searched her hotel room. During questioning, she spoke in a calm, monotone voice, almost as if she was in slow motion.

"I have ended the lives of my two children. I gave them a three-day holiday. A perfect holiday. I knew they were going to take my children to England. It was my intention that my children and me together would go. It wasn't just the children."

She explained that she was certain that Social Services from the United Kingdom would come to take her children away from her. So, she decided it would be better if all three of them were dead than to live their lives apart.

Lianne Smith freely admitted to killing her children and was arrested for double murder by Spanish police.

Later that year, in December 2010, Martin Smith's trial began in Manchester. Despite years of physical and psychological abuse by Martin and knowing that he had repeatedly raped and beaten her children, Lianne testified via video link from her Spanish jail cell and described Martin Smith as a kind and generous man.

During his trial, Sarah waived her right to remain anonymous and testified against him. She told the court how he had repeatedly raped her and attempted to hypnotize her to make her believe it didn't happen. As a result, forty-six-year-old Martin Smith was convicted of eleven counts of rape, attempted rape, indecency with a child, and indecent assault.

Martin Smith was sentenced to sixteen years in jail and could have been released in as little as eight years but, just a few weeks after his conviction, he committed suicide. He was found hanging in his Strangeways prison cell in Manchester.

The following year, Lianne Smith stood trial for the murder of Daniel and Becky. She pleaded guilty on the grounds of diminished responsibility. Her lawyers claimed Lianne was insane. However, a jury of her peers determined that, while she may have been depressed and psychotic, she knew what she was doing. She was convicted and sentenced to thirty-four years in a Spanish prison.

CHAPTER 5
THE GIRL SCOUT

In late January 2002, Brenda van Dam spent the afternoon with her seven-year-old daughter, Danielle, going door to door through their upscale neighborhood in Sabre Springs, California, hoping to sell some Girl Scout cookies.

The neighborhood of Sabre Springs was just twenty minutes north of San Diego and offered a nice, suburban alternative to the hustle and bustle of the city. With newer, large homes, it was an excellent place to raise a family.

Brenda and Danielle had knocked on almost every home in the neighborhood and, on their way home, stopped just two doors away at the house of David Alan Westerfield. Westerfield was a wealthy forty-nine-year-old who worked for himself as a design engineer. He held several patents for medical devices that gave him a nice income. His home and yard were immaculate and large and he often bragged about his luxury motorhome, which he kept parked in the nearby city of Poway.

Westerfield agreed to buy some of Danielle's cookies and chatted with Brenda on his front porch. The two only knew each other in passing, but Westerfield had heard rumors about the lifestyle that Brenda and her husband, Damon, took part in. He had heard that they were swingers.

Brenda and Westerfield engaged in small talk for a while and she mentioned that Damon and their oldest son had planned a trip out of town for a snowboarding weekend.

Brenda also mentioned that she had noticed construction crews in his front yard the year prior, so Westerfield invited them inside to show off his newly remodeled kitchen. As she admired his kitchen, Westerfield said that he'd seen her before at a nearby bar, Dad's Cafe & Steakhouse.

The bar was a favorite of Brenda's. In fact, she told him that she and several of her girlfriends were going there that weekend for a "girl's night out."

Westerfield's ears perked up and he hinted, "If your friends are single, be sure to tell them that you have a rich neighbor you could introduce them to."

However, Brenda got an uneasy feeling from the man when he mentioned that he often had "adult parties" at his home. She wasn't sure exactly what he meant. Was he insinuating that he'd heard that they sometimes had adult parties of their own? Brenda smiled, politely took Danielle's hand, thanked him for buying the cookies, and then left Westerfield's home.

When Brenda and Danielle arrived home, Brenda mentioned Westerfield's odd remark to her husband, Damon, but they both blew it off as nothing. Just a neighbor being weird.

Two nights later, on Friday evening, Brenda's three friends came to their home. The women had a few drinks and smoked a joint in the garage before heading off for their girl's night out. Damon stayed home with Danielle and their two sons, with the kids being sound asleep by 10:00 p.m.

Shortly after the women arrived at Dad's Cafe & Steakhouse, someone bought drinks for them. It was David Westerfield. "Women don't buy their own drinks here," he told them as he tried to strike up a conversation. He and Brenda danced together, but Westerfield grew frustrated when other men in the bar were having more success with the women. As the night progressed, the four girls danced and played pool while Westerfield watched from a distance.

Sometime during the night the four girls snuck out to the car to smoke some more pot and, by 11:00, they noticed Westerfield was gone.

The four women returned to the van Dam residence just after 2:00 a.m. However, when Brenda pulled into the garage she noticed that the home alarm light was blinking because the side door of the garage was open. She closed the door, thinking nothing of it. They had probably left it open when they were there earlier, smoking the joint.

Damon woke when the women got home and they drank some more. Finally, after thirty minutes or so, Brenda's friends went home and she and Damon went to bed.

About an hour later, Damon woke to check on the family dog whimpering by the door. That was when he noticed that another light on the alarm was flashing. This time it was the sliding glass door that led to the backyard. It was cracked open. He, too, assumed that they had mistakenly left the door open and thought nothing of it. He closed the door, reset the alarm, and went back to sleep.

The next morning Brenda, Damon, and the boys woke and Brenda began making breakfast. It was Saturday and Danielle liked to sleep in. By 9:00, however, breakfast was ready and Danielle still hadn't come downstairs. So, Brenda called on one of her boys to wake up their sister – but a few moments later, the boy returned to the kitchen and told his mother, "She's not there."

"What? That's impossible," Brenda said before she trudged up the stairs to find her daughter. She opened the door to Danielle's lavender and pink bedroom only to find her four-poster bed empty. Danielle was indeed gone.

Brenda van Dam was choking and near hysterical when she called 911 at 9:39 a.m. Police immediately sprang into action. A command center was set up in a real estate office nearby and, within hours, hundreds of police and volunteers were helping search for the blue-eyed girl with shoulder-length, blonde hair. By the end of the day, more than 2,000 people were searching for Danielle van Dam.

Volunteers searched through parks and vacant land while police went door to door through the affluent neighborhood, looking for clues. By Saturday evening police had searched more than 200 homes. Every house in the neighborhood… except one. David Westerfield's home.

Westerfield had been the only neighbor that wasn't home that Saturday. He had apparently packed up his luxury motorhome and left for a camping trip just minutes after Brenda had called 911.

Police walked around his property and one officer noticed that a green garden hose seemed out of place. It was stretched out tight across the grass of an otherwise pristine yard. It looked as if he had quickly filled his motorhome with water and left in a hurry.

Police put out an all-points bulletin looking for Westerfield and his RV, but he returned to his home of his own accord two days later, on Monday. When he arrived, the police were there waiting for him.

Westerfield was visibly nervous when he drove home to find police cars in front of his house. Despite the cold February climate, he was sweating profusely and his shirt had large rings of sweat beneath his armpits.

Westerfield gave a detailed description of where he had been over the last few days. He claimed he woke up early that Saturday morning and decided to go camping. He drove his SUV eight miles to Poway, picked up his RV, and then drove it back to his home. He packed the RV with supplies and left the house at about 9:50 a.m.

He explained that he intended to go to the sand dunes in the Imperial County desert east of San Diego but realized he had forgotten his wallet. So, instead, he turned around and went to Silver Strand State Beach, just south of Coronado Island.

He pre-paid for three days in the campground but decided the weather was too cold, so he went back to his home to look for his wallet on Saturday afternoon as police and volunteers frantically searched for Danielle. He told police that a neighbor had told him the girl was missing and he went into his backyard to ensure she hadn't fallen into his pool.

He searched his house for his wallet but eventually realized he had left it in his SUV, parked at the lot in Poway where he usually kept his motorhome. Once he got his wallet, he drove

160 miles east again to the Imperial County desert, as he had initially planned.

Late that night, he explained that his motorhome had gotten stuck in the sand and he'd asked a stranger to dig him out the next day. He then drove to another spot, where he got stuck once again. Frustrated with the desert, Westerfield claimed he drove back to the beach again late on Sunday night, only to find that the gates were closed. He slept in a nearby parking lot, returned the motorhome to its storage space in Poway the following morning, and then drove home in his SUV.

———

Westerfield's story seemed overly elaborate and detailed, with several hundred miles of unnecessary driving. Altogether he listed thirteen different destinations he had driven to, but there were a few things that detectives realized he had omitted from the story. For example, when investigators searched his motorhome they realized it had been thoroughly cleaned. However, Westerfield claimed that was normal. He always cleaned his RV when he returned from a trip. He also omitted a trip to the dry cleaners just before he returned home.

The detectives that interviewed Westerfield noticed that he was overly cooperative: he openly let them search his home and repeatedly apologized for his house being "such a mess," despite it being spotless. The whole place seemed to have been professionally cleaned, with only a few things that weren't immaculate. A comforter was missing from the master bedroom and a load of laundry was on top of the washing machine.

Investigators also noticed that his Toyota 4Runner SUV, which he had parked in the garage, smelled of bleach. Westerfield explained that it had recently been through the car wash as well.

———

Forensic investigators spent the next two and a half weeks analyzing evidence found in Westerfield's home, motorhome, and from the items that he had dropped off for dry cleaning. They also used cell phone records to plot a map of his location during the hours after Danielle had gone missing. It didn't surprise detectives that his cell phone locations didn't match the routes he claimed to have driven that weekend. Instead, the evidence showed that he avoided highways and drove through backroads throughout the desert.

Despite the spotless house and freshly-washed motorhome, the evidence piled up against David Westerfield.

His bedroom sheets, pillowcases, a pair of his boxers, and a lint ball found in the trash contained hairs similar to Danielle's. In addition, the same hairs were found in his bathroom sink drain.

Inside his motorhome, investigators found five tan polyester carpet fibers. Those fibers were found to be the same color, material, and had the same distinctive cross-section pattern as the carpet found in Danielle's bedroom.

On Westerfield's computer, investigators found 64,000 pornographic images; just under 100 of them included underage girls. One particular photo depicted a cartoon image of a frightened young girl begging a man not to rape her.

Twenty-two dog hairs that were similar to Layla, the van Dam's pet Weimaraner, were found throughout Westerfield's house, motorhome, and a comforter that he had dropped off at the dry cleaners. In addition, the lint ball in the trash and a towel on top of his dryer contained eighteen additional dog hairs.

Additionally, investigators found a fingerprint matching Danielle's in his motorhome. The most damning evidence, however, were the droplets of blood found in his motorhome and on a jacket that he had dropped off at the dry cleaners. The blood was a match for Danielle van Dam.

———

For eighteen days, David Westerfield was placed under twenty-four-hour surveillance. Finally, when prosecutors believed they had enough evidence to convict him, detectives arrested Westerfield on February 22, three weeks after Danielle had gone missing. He was initially charged with suspicion of kidnapping and burglary, but the charges would soon include murder. Five days after his arrest, searchers found her body in the desert near Dehesa, California.

Volunteer searchers had learned that Westerfield had avoided highways, so they'd decided to search the back roads leading toward the desert. Just east of El Cajon, they found her body among a group of oak trees that had been a common place for people to dump trash. Her body was just twenty-five feet from the road. The location was eleven miles west of the Sichuan Casino, where Westerfield had a membership to the gaming club.

———

Danielle's body was found nude, indicating that she had most likely been raped before her death. However, the advanced state of decomposition prevented investigators from determining her manner of death.

Danielle was still wearing her favorite plastic choker necklace and Mickey Mouse earrings. Her blue pajamas with yellow flowers lay nearby. Tangled within her hair and necklace were bright orange acrylic fibers. The fibers matched the dozens found in the laundry on top of Westerfield's clothes dryer and the bedding in his laundry. While investigators couldn't find the fibers' source, they believed they had come from a fuzzy blanket or sweater.

Short blue-gray nylon fibers were found beneath her body, on her buttocks. The same fibers were also found in Westerfield's laundry items.

———

Despite the evidence against him, Westerfield insisted he was innocent. He claimed that the child pornography found on his computer must have been downloaded by his eighteen-year-old son, Neal, although his son denied it.

At trial, his lawyers played down the fiber evidence. Instead, they claimed the fibers could have been transferred when Brenda and Danielle came to his house to sell Girl Scout cookies or when Brenda and Westerfield were "dirty dancing" during their encounter at Dad's Cafe & Steakhouse.

The news of the murder and trial became national news. With the media attention, however, Brenda and Damon van Dam's once-private life came into the spotlight. The defense told the court of their marijuana use on the night Danielle went missing and their open relationships with multiple sex partners. They suggested that, because of their open-sex lifestyle, there could have been other people in the house that night that could have abducted Danielle.

Westerfield's defense team also provided expert testimony that stated insect activity on Danielle's body occurred in mid-February, proving that she had only been dead two weeks when she was found. This made it impossible for Westerfield to have killed her since he was under twenty-four-hour surveillance during that time. The prosecution, however, provided conflicting expert testimony from an entomologist that showed insect activity began as early as February 2. This meant Danielle had been killed the same weekend that she went missing.

Westerfield's lawyers also argued that he was improperly interviewed by police for eighteen hours. They claimed he had asked for a lawyer five times, asked to stop the interview four times, inquired about his rights four times, asked to make a telephone call five times, asked for a clean shirt or a shower twice, asked for a drink, and stated he was being abused.

Ultimately, the evidence against Westerfield prevailed. The trial lasted two months and jurors deliberated for ten days before finding him guilty of first-degree murder, kidnapping, and possession of child pornography.

During the penalty phase of Westerfield's trial, his niece, Jenny, testified against him. She told the court that, twelve years earlier when she was seven years old, she and her sister were sleeping at her uncle's home while their parents had gone to a party.

Jenny told the court that she woke up to find Westerfield kneeling beside her bed with his fingers inside her mouth, rubbing her teeth. He then went to her sister's bedside and did the same thing to her. When Westerfield then returned to Jenny's bedside and put his fingers in her mouth again, Jenny bit down as hard as she could. After she bit him, Westerfield stood up, adjusted his running shorts, and left the room.

Jenny's mother, Jeanne, testified about the incident as well. She said that she had confronted Westerfield about his behavior at the time. His excuse was that the girl was fussing in her sleep and he was only comforting her.

On September 16, 2002, the jury recommended a death sentence for David Alan Westerfield. However, due to the 2006 moratorium on executions in California and the July 2014 ruling on the unconstitutionality of the death penalty, it is unlikely he will ever be executed.

———

After the trial had ended, it was reported that, just moments before Danielle's body was discovered, police and Westerfield had agreed upon a plea deal in which he would have revealed the location of the body in exchange for a life sentence without parole.

Audio tapes of Westerfield's initial interrogation were also released, where he can be heard asking the detective to "leave your gun here for a few minutes," suggesting he wanted to commit suicide.

The van Dam family was awarded $416,000 from several insurance companies which had insured Westerfield's home, motorhome, and SUV.

Today, just a few miles from where her body was found, an overpass on Interstate 8 has been named the Danielle van Dam Memorial Overpass.

CHAPTER 6
WHERE'S SAVANNA?

The Greywind family were members of the Spirit Lake Tribe of Native Americans and lived most of their life on the Spirit Lake Dakota Reservation in east-central North Dakota, on the south side of Devils Lake. But when Joe and Norberta's daughter, Savanna, wanted to go to nursing school, they were more than willing to help.

Twenty-two-year-old Savanna Greywind was the eldest of four children in the tight-knit family. So, Joe and Norberta decided that rather than send Savanna away to school, they would pack up the whole family and move three hours southeast to Fargo, North Dakota.

However, one of the downsides to the move was that Savanna would be moving away from her longtime boyfriend, Ashton Matheny. Savanna and Ashton had been together since she was sixteen, despite her agreement with her parents that she wouldn't date until she was eighteen. But seven years had gone by and Savanna and Ashton were still very much in love. It was hard for her to move away, but they had no intention of breaking up because of a three-hour drive between them. Ashton worked construction and often traveled for work. Thus, after the move, they spoke on the telephone almost daily and saw each other every chance they could.

In early 2017, the couple found themselves pregnant. It wasn't the ideal situation but Savanna, Ashton, and the Greywind family couldn't have been more excited to welcome a baby girl into the family. While attending school, Savanna still lived with her parents and family but everyone was prepared to help the young couple. Ashton planned to move to Fargo and they would soon get their own apartment near the family and Savanna's school.

————

The Greywind family lived in a basement apartment in a three-story building on the north side of Fargo. Although the family was acquainted with the tenants in the building, they weren't very close to any of them. They had said "hello" when passing in the hallways or outside the building, but there weren't any neighbors they would really call friends.

That was why it was such a surprise when a woman that lived on the third floor knocked on the Greywinds' door. Savanna answered; the woman wanted to see if she was interested in coming upstairs to her apartment to smoke some pot with her.

It was August and Savanna was eight months pregnant. Of course she didn't want to smoke pot with the woman. Savanna politely declined her offer and closed the door. The woman was thirty-nine-year-old Brooke Crews, who shared an upstairs apartment with her boyfriend, thirty-three-year-old William Hoehn. Savanna really didn't know much about her other than that she lived in the same building.

A few days later, in the early afternoon of Saturday, August 19, Savanna was home alone when there was a knock on the door. It was Brooke Crews again. This time Brooke had an offer for Savanna. Brooke explained that she was sewing a dress and wanted Savanna to try it on for her. Was it a maternity dress? It must have been. Brooke said it wouldn't take long and she would pay her $20 for her time. Savanna agreed.

Savanna sent her mother a text telling her she had ordered a pizza for the family's lunch and would run upstairs to apartment five for a bit. She then sent another text to Ashton and followed Brooke Crews upstairs.

———

When Norberta Greywind returned home from running errands, Savanna had not returned. Norberta sent her son upstairs to check on her, but the son returned and told his mother that the lady upstairs said they were still working on the dress.

When Savanna's father, Joe, returned home from work an hour later, she still wasn't home. Joe climbed the stairs to apartment number five and knocked on the door.

When Brooke answered the door and Joe asked to speak to his daughter, Brooke explained that she was in the back room trying on the dress and that she would be back down shortly.

But when another hour passed and Savanna still hadn't returned, he went to the upstairs apartment again. This time she claimed Savanna had already left.

"Where'd she go?" he asked.

Brooke told him that Savanna had gone home but he knew that wasn't true. Joe immediately knew there was something wrong.

He asked,

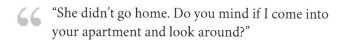 "She didn't go home. Do you mind if I come into your apartment and look around?"

Brooke flatly told him no and closed the door. The hairs on the back of Joe's neck stood on end. He knew something terrible had happened. Savanna's car was still in the driveway and her wallet was still in their apartment. Where could she have possibly gone? She was eight months pregnant, after all.

———

Norberta Greywind called the police at 4:27 that afternoon and explained their situation. She told police that Savanna was not the type to just vanish – especially in her condition.

Police arrived at 5:00, went up to Brooke's apartment, and knocked on the door. Brooke and William answered the door and welcomed the officers into their apartment. Brooke was in a cheerful mood and again explained that Savanna had left quite a while ago; she had no idea where she had gone. The officers went room to room through the apartment but, besides being horribly messy, they saw no sign of a struggle or a crime.

The officers returned to the Greywinds' apartment and explained that they found nothing out of the ordinary in the upstairs apartment. Savanna wasn't there.

When Savanna hadn't returned by 10:00 p.m., the Greywind family was frantic and called the police again. They insisted that officers search the upstairs apartment again. Their daughter couldn't have just disappeared and they knew she was last seen with Brooke Crews.

Police arrived a second time and, again, Brooke and William welcomed them into their home. The officers went through the rooms of the small apartment, saw nothing out of the ordinary, and again came downstairs to report their findings to the Greywind family.

Worried sick about their daughter and granddaughter, the entire family got no sleep that night. The next day they called the police a third time.

The third time police knocked on apartment number five's door, they had two detectives with them. Brooke and William welcomed them in a third time and, again, they found nothing. Just an extremely messy apartment with boxes, garbage, clothing, and miscellaneous items strewn everywhere, but no sign of Savanna.

———

Law enforcement, family, and friends got together to search for Savanna. Ashton had been housesitting for his mother eighty miles north in Grand Forks and drove down to help with the search. They put up flyers all over town and contacted the media. All calls to Savanna's cell phone went unanswered.

Police held a press conference and asked the public to check any vacant buildings, empty residences, and even dumpsters in the area.

Tips came in of possible sightings of Savanna, but only one was of any use. An anonymous tipster claimed they thought they saw her getting into a red truck.

————

Detectives brought both Williams Hoehn and Brooke Crews in for questioning and placed them in separate interrogation rooms.

Brooke stuck to her same story. She explained that Savanna had left her home at 2:45 p.m. that afternoon and was healthy and walking on her own two feet.

William told police that he had come home from work and Brooke briefly introduced him to Savanna before he went into the bedroom, turned on his computer, and took a shower. When he came out of the shower, she was gone.

————

When police questioned a woman who lived on the second floor of the apartment complex and asked if she knew anyone who owned a red truck, the woman told detectives that the man upstairs drove a red truck – William Hoehn, in apartment five. In fact, he had parked it at the back of the apartment building on the day Savanna had gone missing.

When questioned about the truck, William admitted that he sometimes drove a red Chevy Silverado but it wasn't his. It belonged to his boss, but he claimed he hadn't been driving it the day Savanna went missing.

To follow up on his claim, detectives spoke to William's employer. His boss owned the roofing company that William worked for and had a different story. He said that William did have the truck that day – but the next thing he said stepped up the police's concern. His boss told police that William had mentioned that he and Brooke had just had a baby.

————

Detectives put both William Hoehn and Brooke Crews under twenty-four-hour surveillance. On August 22, police arrested William Hoehn on an unrelated outstanding warrant after they followed him to Walmart, where they watched him buy diapers. They arrested him as he returned home but he was out on bail within hours.

Two days later, Brooke Crews locked her apartment door and pushed a couch in front of it when she saw a swarm of police cars screeching to a stop on the street below her apartment. Police used a battering ram to knock down the door of apartment number five and took her into custody. A tiny infant with messy black hair was lying in between pillows on their bed.

Emergency crews rushed the four-pound, eleven-ounce baby to the hospital. Amazingly, she was safe and healthy, but the Greywind family were not allowed to see her until DNA proved the baby's identity. Unfortunately, there was still no sign of Savanna.

William Hoehn was arrested shortly afterward at his job site. Inside their apartment, authorities found midwifery notes, a list of items to buy to deliver a baby, and various letters and journals belonging to Brooke Crews. The notes showed evidence that she had tried to convince William that she could conceive his baby despite already having had a hysterectomy. There was proof that she had begun faking a pregnancy and lying to him for months.

Looking into Brooke Crews' background, investigators discovered her history of abandoning children. She already had seven children of her own from five different men. At the time of Savanna's death, Crews had no contact with her own children and owed child support for two of them. In addition, one of the fathers of her children reported that she had a habit of leaving children when they reached a certain age.

William Hoehn had a backstory as well. He was the father of two children with whom he had very little contact – one he had physically abused, fracturing their skull.

Brooke Crews stuck to her story. She was confrontational and told police that Savanna was fine when she left her house at 2:45. However, when detectives told her that her boyfriend was in another interrogation room telling them what really happened, she started to change her story.

William Hoehn told detectives that he knew they were going to prison and needed to "cover his ass." He pointed the blame squarely at Brooke. He claimed that, for the last several months, he believed that Brooke was pregnant with their baby. Brooke had told him of the doctor's visits and the beating heart inside her. He told detectives he had no idea she wasn't pregnant until he came home from work on August 19 to find Savanna Greywind bleeding on the bathroom floor and a baby in the bedroom.

Knowing what William was telling detectives, Brooke changed her story. She said that Savanna was in her apartment when she suddenly went into labor and delivered the baby. After she gave birth, Brooke claimed, Savanna handed the baby to her and told her she didn't want it. She claimed Savanna then left the apartment and that she didn't know where she went.

Detectives, of course, didn't believe her story for a minute and told her,

 "They're gonna find her blood in your goddamn apartment!"

Brooke screamed back that they were wrong.

Neither William nor Brooke, however, gave any indication as to the whereabouts or current condition of Savanna Greywind. Still, investigators knew they were now looking for a body.

———

Hundreds of volunteers took to the vast wilderness throughout Fargo to search for Savanna. Three days later, two kayakers paddling north on the Red River came across a large object stuck on a log. It was wrapped in black plastic garbage bags, tightened with duct tape, and reeked of decomposition. When police arrived, they pulled the body of Savanna Greywind from the river.

———

The pathologist couldn't determine whether Savanna had died from strangulation from the rope tied around her neck or from blood loss due to the gaping wound across her abdomen that spanned from hip to hip.

———

On August 29, Ashton and the Greywind family were allowed to meet the adorable new addition to their family, Haisley Jo Matheny. Unfortunately, they were simultaneously mourning the loss of Savanna.

———

Prosecutors knew that there was no way either one of them had killed Savanna on their own. After repeated interrogations by detectives, Brooke Crews pleaded guilty to conspiracy to commit murder, conspiracy to commit kidnapping, and lying to police. In February 2018, Brooke Crews was sentenced to life in prison without the possibility of parole.

In September 2018, William Hoehn pleaded guilty to conspiracy to commit kidnapping and providing false information to police. Still, he insisted he had nothing to do with the murder and pleaded innocent.

William Hoehn was tried on the charge of conspiracy to commit murder in September 2018 and Brooke Crews testified against him. She painted a picture of him as an abusive partner who desperately wanted a baby. She said that he was telling people she was pregnant and demanded that she produce a baby by any means. It didn't matter how she got it.

She said that when Hoehn saw how pregnant Savanna was, he said to her, "That Greywind girl is really pregnant," insinuating that she should steal her baby.

Crews claimed that she was still alive when she sliced Savanna open but that Hoehn finished the job. She told the court that Hoehn put the rope around her neck, pulled it tight, and said,

 "If she wasn't dead before, she is now."

Ultimately, the jury didn't buy her story and William Hoehn was found not guilty of conspiracy to commit murder. However, due to his guilty plea of conspiracy to commit kidnapping, he was still going to jail.

The kidnapping conviction carried a maximum of twenty years in prison – but, because of Hoehn's prior child abuse conviction in 2012, Case County prosecutors designated him a dangerous special offender. With the extra charge, he was sentenced to life behind bars.

Hoehn's attorneys, however, filed an appeal to the sentence and argued that the dangerous special offender charge had been misapplied. As a result, in 2019 his sentence was reduced to 21 years minus 775 days for the time he had already served.

———

Further interrogations, court proceedings, and later interviews with reporters revealed that Brooke Crews lured Savanna to the apartment. Once she was there, Brooke instigated an argument with her, accusing her of harassing her cat. As they fought, Crews grabbed her hair and smashed her head against the bathroom sink.

With Savanna still alive on the bathroom floor, she took a utility knife and sliced her abdomen from hip to hip. Then, she removed the baby and left Savanna to bleed out on the bathroom floor.

According to Brooke, William Hoehn then strangled her with a rope. He denied this claim, so it's a matter of he-said, she-said.

During the first three police searches, Hoehn told investigators that the baby was lying on the bed the whole time. The officers just never noticed because she was silent and blended in with the messy apartment.

Also during the three searches, the body of Savanna Greywind was packed in plastic garbage bags and duct tape in a closet in the bathroom as they walked through. The police glanced briefly into the bathroom each time and moved along.

On August 21, just before Hoehn was arrested the first time, they packed the body of Savanna Greywind into a dresser that he had hollowed out. He managed to carry the dresser down three flights of stairs and into the red Chevy Silverado without anyone seeing. Then, in the middle of the night, he drove to a bridge crossing the Red River and dumped the dresser over the edge.

Police records also revealed that when Hoehn and Crews were under surveillance and officers watched as they shopped for diapers at Walmart, the tiny baby was in a shopping bag that Crews was carrying. When they arrived home and detectives arrested Hoehn, Crews was watching his arrest while holding the bag with the baby in it.

Hailey Jo Matheny is five years old at the time of this writing and the Greywind family regularly post updates on a Facebook page, showing her smiling face. Unfortunately, they have no idea how they will ever explain the events to her.

CHAPTER 7
THE IHOP MURDER

Dee Dyne Casteel was born in 1938 in Tampa, Florida, to an alcoholic mother and a father who only stuck around for the first year of her life. Dee's mother did her best to raise her on her own, but she was diagnosed with tuberculosis and sent to a sanitarium just a few years after she gave birth. Dee was sent to live with her grandmother for the next several years.

Years later, after her mother's death, Dee's father remarried and wanted her to live with them. It was in her teens that her father taught her how to bowl and she eventually became one of the top female bowlers in Florida.

In high school Dee blossomed into a beautiful girl. She had a happy childhood, did well in school, became a cheerleader, and sang in the school choir. Her father and stepmother bought her a brand-new car on her seventeenth birthday – but seventeen was also when she started to become a wild child.

When the car arrived, the drinking began. She found a love for alcohol that would follow her for most of her life. The freedom the vehicle provided and the excessive alcohol led to an unplanned pregnancy the same year. Her boyfriend, Harry, had agreed to marry her but backed out at the last minute, leaving her at the altar. Harry later came around and the pair eventually married, but the marriage lasted only briefly.

Dee's father and stepmother knew that an unwed teen mother with no job skills didn't stand a chance in life, so they agreed to raise Dee's son as their own. Then her parents sent her to college to complete her high school equivalency and build her secretarial skills.

She landed a job with the city of Hialeah where she worked as an executive secretary for the popular mayor, Henry Milander, who was re-elected for eight terms.

Milander took Dee under his wing and introduced her to Florida's political figures, business leaders, and millionaires. As a result, the young, beautiful woman dated wealthy men who owned large beachfront homes and yachts. These men took her to the best nightclubs and restaurants and lavished her with expensive gifts – but Dee was only interested in them if they were drinkers. If a suitor didn't drink, they usually wouldn't get a second date from Dee.

While dating a wealthy businessman from Miami, Dee got pregnant again. But rather than trying to get the man to marry her, this time Dee asked him to pay for an abortion. Much to her surprise, however, he refused. It was Mayor Milander who saw the potential in his young mentee and gave her the money to pay for the abortion.

The stigma of the abortion and her excessive drinking followed Dee everywhere she went. She worked briefly as an executive secretary for Florida Power and Light, but she was let go when they heard rumors of her drunkenness and the abortion.

A similar situation emerged when she became a pro bowler in the Women's International Bowling Conference. Dee wasn't a good match for what the league was looking for in a role model and her bowling career ended abruptly.

When Dee was twenty-eight years old, she married a second time. Her new husband, Lester, was a heavy drinker like herself, but he was an angry drunk. He often became abusive during his drunken bouts. Dee and Lester had a baby together and she stopped drinking for a year during the pregnancy. However, the marriage ended when Lester put a gun to her head in a drunken argument. She took her daughter and left him.

Dee met her third husband while working as a Dade county police dispatcher. She and Charlie White met at a party when they were drunk and slept together on their first meeting. Charlie, too, was an alcoholic who installed air conditioning units, but when he was diagnosed with kidney disease he couldn't work for a year.

Eventually, Dee lost her job with Dade county when they ran a background check and found out about her excessive alcoholism. Later that year she worked in the billing department of Miller Gas. Dee, however, had been stealing from the company. In her mind, she only considered it borrowing since she planned on paying it back. However, by the time the sum grew to more than $14,000, there was no way she could pay it back. When the company learned of her theft, they decided to avoid having her arrested and she escaped with only the loss of her job.

Dee and Charlie inevitably divorced, after which she met her next husband, Cass, while working as a bartender at the Saga Lounge.

Dee drank more and more and alcohol had completely taken over her life by her mid-thirties. Her drink of choice was scotch and she could polish off three bottles a day single-handedly. Eventually, the only job she could get was working as a waitress or bartending and even then she found it hard to keep a job. She was inevitably caught drinking on the job and was fired from the Saga Lounge. Over the years she had become well-known at the restaurants and dive bars in the area, meaning no one wanted to hire her.

———

By early 1983 Dee Casteel had worked as a waitress at the International House of Pancakes for nine months and was sure she would be fired again. She knew the manager, Alan Bryant, had seen the bottle of scotch she'd stashed in the back room. Every day she mixed the scotch into the iced coffee that she sipped all day long. It was the only way she could get through the day. She was surprised that Alan had never said a word about it.

However, the day after he found the bottle, Dee was convinced she would be fired. She had even brought her extra waitress uniform with her, prepared to turn it in at the end of her shift. Sure enough, when Alan walked into the IHOP that morning he told Dee to grab her coat. They were going for a drive.

Although Alan Bryant was twenty years younger than forty-five-year-old Dee, she found herself magnetically attracted to him. It didn't matter that he was flamboyant, effeminate, and openly gay. All her life Dee had been attracted to large, burly men, most of whom had physically abused her. Alan was the polar opposite, which was why it surprised her that she had such a crush on him. She saw him as a polite, southern gentleman.

Dee grabbed her purse and left the IHOP with Alan, fully prepared to be fired for drinking on the job. As they drove, Dee's eyes widened with surprise when Alan said he knew about her drinking on the job and said he didn't care. It was okay.

Alan was more interested in getting his love life frustrations off his chest. He needed to talk. Alan was sick of his current lover, Art Venecia, and had been cheating on him with his new boyfriend, Henry Ramos – a young, good-looking, Cuban immigrant. His relationship with Art had run its course, and he was ready to end it. Art was twenty years older, they argued all the time, and Alan referred to him as "the old fuddy-duddy."

———

Art Venecia and Alan Bryant had been dating for several years. Alan had worked in restaurants for years before they met, and Art had purchased the IHOP specifically to give Alan a project to run. Something to keep him busy. Art was a forty-five-year-old successful businessman and had worked hard his entire life. He'd saved for retirement and owned a home, a restaurant, a thirty-five-foot yacht, and various other businesses and real estate.

Alan, however, was not a hard worker at all. He was a taker. A leech. Always looking for whatever he could get with the least amount of work possible. When they first started dating, Art thought he could change Alan – but almost everything Alan did was for the benefit of himself alone. He habitually lied to those around him and had a problem with pills and alcohol.

Art had given Alan everything he needed to run the restaurant, including a company car and allowing him to take money from the cash register. Alan, however, constantly took more money than was agreed upon, leaving the restaurant short. Although Art rarely came to the restaurant, when he did, the employees usually heard the two screaming at each other in the upstairs office. On more than one occurrence, employees saw Art leaving the office with scratch marks on his face.

———

As Alan complained about Art and drove Dee through the streets of Dade county, he spontaneously asked her, "I heard you know somebody who can 'take a contract.' Like a hired killer. Is that true?"

Dee, who had already had a few drinks that morning, chuckled, assuming Alan was joking. However, when she looked into his eyes she realized he was serious.

 "Oh, wow. Well, yeah, I know a guy who's always telling me he could take care of my husband for me, but I always figured it was just his strange way of flirting with me. I don't know if he's really ever done something like that, but I can ask… if you're serious? Is that something you're really considering?"

"Yes, really. I just need to get rid of him. That way, I can be with Henry and not feel guilty about it."

Dee was flabbergasted at his request but, at the same time, she was flattered that he trusted her. She wanted so badly to make Alan happy. Her attraction to him, coupled with now having a job where she could drink while she worked, motivated her. She was willing to do anything for him. Dee told Alan she would talk to her guy and see what he said.

———

Forty-three-year-old Michael Irvine worked as a mechanic at a local Amoco gas station and had been friends with Dee's current husband, Cass, for years. It was common knowledge that Dee's marriage was on the rocks and Mike had often joked that he could get rid of Cass for her.

That evening, Dee stopped by the gas station and mentioned to Mike that she might be interested in his proposition. Mike stopped her before she said any more and told her to come to his apartment at 3:00 in the morning, where they could have a few drinks and talk some more.

Dee showed up as promised and she and Mike sat in her car, drank scotch, and talked business. Dee explained that it wasn't for her; it was for a friend. Without a thought, Mike quipped,

 "I bet it's that queer bastard you work for. He probably wants to off his boyfriend."

Mike admitted that he'd never really done anything like that. Mike wasn't a career criminal at all – he had been arrested for drugs and petty theft a few times, but nothing serious. Mike told Dee he couldn't do the job himself but he might know someone who could.

He told Dee that he would need a photo of Art and his day-to-day schedule, so he could talk to his guy and get back to her with a price to do the job.

When Dee relayed the news to Alan at work the next day, he was excited. He gave her a passport photo of Art and told her that he was usually drunk and asleep by 11:00 p.m. every night, so they could kill him in his house at night.

The following night Dee met with Mike again and gave him the photo and info. Mike said that his friend could do it for $2,500, half up front and the other half once the job was done. Dee assured Mike that the money wouldn't be a problem; Alan would pay.

A few days later, while Mike and his friend prepared to do the job, Alan asked Dee to go for another drive.

Alan drove toward Fort Lauderdale and said to Dee, "I was thinking… why should we pay them when we can do it ourselves?" He said he knew a place in Fort Lauderdale where they could buy a gun.

Dee was shocked, "Wait a minute! I'm not going to kill anyone!" But Alan reassured her he would pull the trigger and he only needed her help picking out a gun. Alan had never handled a firearm and barely knew how they worked. Dee, however, had been married to four men, all of whom were avid hunters. As a result, she knew much more about guns than Alan ever would.

Alan and Dee drank scotch as they drove to the Fort Lauderdale gun store, where Dee picked out a .32 caliber pistol that would do the job. They told the store owner they wanted the gun, a small leather holster, and some ammunition. However, when the owner rang up the sale, Alan claimed he had forgotten his wallet. He had the cash in hand but he conveniently didn't bring any identification. That meant they would have to buy the gun in Dee's name. Dee wasn't crazy about having a murder weapon registered in her name. Still, she didn't want to disappoint Alan and reluctantly agreed.

That night, Alan and Dee drove through the backroads of southern Florida, drinking scotch and shooting the gun out the car window.

Alan shot at beer bottles and road signs through the night until he decided he was ready to kill Art. Although they were so drunk they could barely stand, let alone drive, they pulled up to Art's home. Alan tucked the gun into his pants and went inside, intent on ending his lover's life. Dee couldn't see straight and lay down on the sidewalk outside.

When Alan came out of the house, Dee was passed out on the sidewalk. He woke her up, helped her back into the car, and told her he couldn't do it. "Let's just have your friends do it."

———

A few days later, Alan took $1,250 out of the cash register of the IHOP, handed it to Dee, and told her to take it to Mike Irvine. Again, Dee met with Mike late at night and gave him the cash. Mike told her that he and his friend Bil Rhodes, who also worked at the Amoco station, would murder Art sometime over the following weekend – Friday or Saturday night. As Dee spoke with Mike, however, she had a feeling that the murder would never really happen.

When Alan found out the possible dates of the murder, he made reservations to take a trip to Orlando for the weekend. He wanted to be as far away as possible to give himself a solid alibi.

———

On Sunday, June 13, 1994, Dee worked the morning shift at the IHOP. She started drinking early that day because she knew that, if everything went as planned, Art was dead already. She scanned the headlines as soon as the Miami Herald was delivered that morning, but there was no news about a murder. Each time the phone rang she jumped. She was sure there would be news of the murder. However, Dee was both surprised and a bit relieved when she saw Art walk in the front door that afternoon and enter the office to review the restaurant's books.

When Alan called the store, he was furious to find out that the job hadn't gone down. He demanded to know what went wrong. Alan knew that if Art was still alive and going through the books, he would have also known the money was missing from the safe. Alan had taken $1,600 from the restaurant's safe for his trip to Orlando. The money should have been deposited the Friday before, and now the checks written to vendors would bounce.

When Alan returned to the IHOP from his weekend in Orlando, he and Art disappeared into the office. Both customers and employees cringed when they heard the screaming coming out.

Dee ended her shift and went home for the evening but received a call late that night from Art.

When Art asked if Alan had given her $1,600 to pay for her divorce, Dee was confused. Alan lied to him and said he had taken the money from the cash register to help Dee. Although Dee initially had no idea what he was talking about, she was quick on her feet and told him that Alan had given her the money.

Art also let Dee know that Alan had been admitted to the hospital that night. He had attempted suicide by swallowing a handful of pills and was having his stomach pumped.

Regardless of Alan's condition, Art was infuriated and fired him. He told Dee to inform the other employees that Alan was no longer allowed in the IHOP.

With Alan and Art broken up, Dee felt an enormous relief that the murder wouldn't happen. On the downside, however, Alan would no longer be running the IHOP, and she would have to hide her drinking on the job again. So while Alan was in the hospital, Dee drove to visit Mike and let him know that the murder was off.

The next afternoon Alan was released from the hospital and checked himself into a hotel. Dee visited him at the hotel and brought scotch and some of his clothes – but when she told him that she had told Mike the murder was canceled, he was furious.

Alan asked why on Earth she had canceled the murder. She explained that, because he and Art were broken up, he could move in with Henry and he didn't have to worry about Art anymore. Alan scoffed and told her none of that mattered. He still wanted him dead.

Art was his meal ticket. Alan had no savings and, without a job, he had no way to live. Dee didn't quite understand why he still wanted Art dead but, to appease him, she called Mike back and told him the murder for hire was still on.

Mike told Dee it would cost $5,000 now and Alan agreed. Alan planned to steal the money from Art anyway. Mike also told Alan there was a new stipulation – Alan needed to come with them during the job. Again, Alan had no problem with that. That night Dee and Alan drank scotch in the hotel room until they passed out.

By the next afternoon, everything had changed. Art had felt sorry for Alan. Finally, they made up and Art hired him back as manager of the IHOP and handed back the keys to the company car. But that didn't change any of Alan's plans; he still wanted him dead.

On Wednesday, June 15, 1983, Alan gave Dee an envelope containing $2,500 in twenty dollar bills. This was money that he had, again, stolen from the IHOP. Dee drove the money to Mike, who reminded her that Alan would need to come with them on the night of the murder.

Mike again hired his co-worker Bil Rhodes. Bil was short, stocky, and muscular. He had been in the Air Force and then spent a few years in prison for breaking and entering. He always carried a box-cutter knife in his pocket and went by the nickname "The Joker."

———

Alan and Dee sat in a booth at the IHOP on the evening of Saturday, June 18, as they waited for Mike and Bil to arrive. They arrived on time at 11:30 and Alan left with them while Dee waited at the IHOP, drinking and chewing her fingernails. Forty minutes later the car returned. Alan got out, came into the IHOP, and told Dee it was done. Art was dead.

Art had been asleep when Alan let the two men into his home. Bil and Mike walked into the bedroom and attacked. Although Art did his best to fight off his assailants, it was no use. They overpowered him as Art's feet tangled in his bed sheets. Mike held him down while Bil slashed his throat with the box cutter. Art Venecia bled out on the bedroom floor.

———

The next day was Father's Day and a busy morning at the IHOP. After the breakfast rush, Dee and Alan went to Art's house to clean up the mess, but it was worse than she had imagined. The bedroom was covered in blood. They scrubbed the room and dragged Art's body to the air-conditioned garage, then turned the temperature down as far as it could go.

Dee and Alan crammed Art's body and the bloody linens from the bedroom into a large wooden wardrobe. As they cleaned the house, Dee noticed a trailer at the front of the property and Alan explained that Art's eighty-three-year-old mother, Bessie, lived there. Dee was shocked. She had no idea that Art's mother lived on the property. Who would take care of her?

Alan was unconcerned and told Dee that she was senile. He could tell her that Art was in North Carolina on business. She would never even remember if he'd said goodbye to her before he left.

Dee wasn't okay with that. She worried about Bessie, especially when Alan suggested she could call Mike again and have him take care of her, too. She didn't want any part in the killing of an elderly lady.

Dee walked over to the trailer and introduced herself to Bessie. She explained that Art was away on business and she would be bringing her meals while he was gone. Every morning and evening, Dee brought her a meal from the IHOP. Meanwhile, Alan disconnected Bessie's telephone and changed the locks on Art's house. He didn't want her snooping around.

The following week, Alan gathered the IHOP employees and told them that Art was looking to buy another restaurant in North Carolina. He made Dee assistant manager of the IHOP and told her that she would be handling the day-to-day operations. From that point forward, Alan rarely came to the restaurant except to take money from the register.

Art's body had been in the garage for a week when Alan decided they needed to move the wardrobe to a small barn on another part of the property. To ensure Bessie didn't watch, Dee dropped her off at a beauty shop to get her hair done while she and Alan moved the wardrobe to the barn.

Like clockwork, Dee showed up twice a day to bring Bessie her meals, often sitting with her to chat while she ate. Besides visiting with Dee, Bessie only watched soap operas and game shows with her cat. Every day she asked about her son and each time Dee made up lies about his business dealings in North Carolina.

Each day Dee drove onto the property, the smell of decomposition in the hot, humid, Florida summer sun seemed worse and worse.

Art's body had been rotting for weeks before Dee and Alan walked into the barn. The smell was overwhelming and bodily fluids were leaking out of the wardrobe. Something needed to be done.

Dee had been working long hours now that she was running the restaurant and her drinking had gotten heavier and heavier. Alan had rented a house and moved in with his new boyfriend. Alan added air conditioning, new carpeting, appliances, and a new deck despite it being a rental home – all with the money he stole from the IHOP and Art's investment accounts, which he had been accessing. He even bought his boyfriend a new car.

However, Alan was still concerned about the loose end... Bessie. He repeatedly told Dee that she needed to go. He tried to reason with her, explaining that she was old and would die soon anyway. He told her they would actually be doing her a favor if they had her killed, since she would die without knowing that her son had been murdered.

But Dee hated his suggestions. Each time he brought it up, she argued and pleaded with him not to do it. She had become friends with her. But, deep down, Dee knew it would happen.

When Dee was arrested for DUI while driving home from a long day of work, she went to Alan for consolation. Alan insisted that she was only drinking more because of the stress of Bessie still being around to find out what they had done. He reasoned that if Bessie was gone, her anxiety would magically disappear.

Alan often took Dee out to nice dinners and the two of them would dress up. Dee loved it. He bought her gifts, gave her a raise, and always supplied her with endless scotch. She felt like they were actually dating, which was precisely what she wanted. Of course, Alan was only trying to change her mind about Bessie. Dee's infatuation with Alan eventually got the best of her. She wanted so desperately to please him that, finally, she agreed to talk to Mike about getting rid of Bessie.

Mike told Dee it would cost $2,500 to get rid of Bessie Fischer. Again, half up front, half when the job was done. Alan agreed to the price but Dee insisted that she didn't want it to be messy this time. Plus, getting rid of the body needed to be included in the price.

Six weeks had passed since the death of Art Venecia and the smell emanating from the barn had become unbearable. When Alan rented a small backhoe and tried to dig a hole on the property, he realized that beneath the topsoil was solid coral. There was no getting through it without bigger equipment.

Dee called Wayne Tidwell, who owned a professional backhoe service. She told him she needed a large trash pit dug on the southeast corner of the property. Wayne noticed the horrible smell coming from the barn right away, but Dee explained that it was just a lot of trash to get rid of.

Within days Wayne Tidwell had dug an eighteen-foot, square pit that was four feet deep. It was more than large enough to bury two bodies.

———

At 5:00 p.m. on Saturday, August 6, 1983, Dee brought Bessie a club sandwich, peach cobbler, and iced tea from the IHOP. She sat with Bessie while she ate and they talked about the leaky roof on her trailer. Dee explained that some men would come to fix the roof in a few minutes and she should let them come in. As Dee drove down the driveway, she saw

Bil and Mike driving toward the trailer. Mike winked at her as their cars passed.

Bessie did as she was told and let the men into her home. Mike watched as Bil strangled her with a nylon stocking in the kitchen.

The next day Mike stopped by the IHOP to pick up the rest of the money and told Dee the job was done. But the following day, when she and Alan went into the trailer, Bessie's body was still in the kitchen chair, her head slumped toward her chest. They hadn't buried her as they had said they would do.

Dee was upset and drove to the Amoco station and told Bil that they didn't hold up their end of the bargain. They still needed to bury her. But Bil snapped back, "I don't plant 'em; I only kill 'em." Three days later, however, Bil and Mike returned to the trailer and threw her body into the trash pit.

Again, Alan rented a backhoe and a forklift, then he and Dee moved the wardrobe with Alan's body in it into the trash pit. However, when he tried to move the slabs of coral back into the hole, the backhoe wasn't powerful enough. Instead, he covered the bodies in the bottom of the trash pit with a king-sized mattress and some trash, then Dee called Wayne Tidwell again to fill in the pit.

———

In mid-August, friends of Art's from out of town were driving through south Florida and decided to stop by. When they got there they were met by Dee, who told them he was out of town on business. They were instantly suspicious, though. Art had been a meticulous housekeeper and gardener. He loved to raise orchids, but Art's orchids and other plants were dead and the yard had been overtaken with weeds. Art would never have allowed his yard to look so bad.

———

With Art and Bessie out of the way, Alan began liquidating everything Art had owned. He rifled through his retirement account and forged and cashed dividend checks.

Alan was still taking money from the register at the IHOP to the tune of $3,000 a week, but that meant the restaurant wasn't making enough to pay its suppliers and the franchise fees due to the International House of Pancakes main office. Dee begged him to pay the franchise fees but he wouldn't listen.

Although Dee was still in love with Alan, she was frustrated that she wasn't making enough money to survive. When she was eventually evicted from her apartment, Alan suggested she and her two boys should move into Art's house. It was just sitting there.

At Alan's instruction, Dee placed an ad in the newspaper to sell Bessie's trailer for $4,000.

Just a month after Bessie's murder, Dee, her sons, and her daughter, Susan, moved into Art's house. She had recently divorced her husband but Dee was still stressed and drinking more than ever.

After a night of binge drinking with her daughter, Dee admitted that she was madly in love with Alan. Her daughter tried to reason with her, "For Christ's sake, he's gay!" But Dee insisted, "People change. He's all I have and he gives me attention."

By October, Alan was still going through Art's possessions and systematically selling them, but he realized he could get money for its equity if he refinanced Art's house. So Alan talked Dee into acting as a broker, while Alan posed as Art. Remarkably, they were able to refinance the home without showing any identification at all.

Alan was spending money as quickly as he could get it. He sold Art's yacht for $36,000 and an antique organ that Art had been restoring for $14,000. The bills, however, were going unpaid. The company car had been repossessed and, in January 1984, the IHOP was repossessed by the corporate office.

Not everybody bought the story that Art was still away on business, buying another restaurant in North Carolina when the restaurant he had in Florida had gone under. Ann Smith, one of the employees from the IHOP, had become suspicious. She had stopped by Art's home and noticed its terrible condition. As her suspicions grew, she called the North Carolina Hotel and Restaurant Association to see if she could reach Art, but they had no record of Art in any negotiations to buy a restaurant.

By February, Art's house had become dilapidated and Alan was determined to sell it before it was taken by the bank. Alan became a notary public and forged documents to give Dee power of attorney for Art. Together they sold the house for $120,000, but after the mortgage was paid off there was only $15,000 left. Alan gave Dee $3,500 to help her get an apartment but, without a job and drinking three bottles a day, she was spiraling down the drain. It was finally starting to sink in that she would never get Alan to fall in love with her.

In early spring 1984, Dee sat her daughter, Susan, and her friend, Jackie Reagan, down at the kitchen table after a particularly heavy drinking binge. She instructed Susan to write down everything she said. Finally, she was ready to come clean. She told her what she was writing down was her "life insurance." She was worried that, now that there was nothing left to sell, she too would become a liability to Alan and he may someday want to have her killed. So, she told Susan and Jackie everything, from start to finish.

Days later, Jackie Reagan relayed what Dee had confessed to Ann Smith, who promptly went to the police with the information. The police, however, ignored her initial calls. There was no evidence of a crime except for a drunken confession to friends. However, when she told them that the barn had once housed the body of Art Venecia, they decided to take a look. As soon as they entered the barn, they saw a massive stain of what seemed to be bodily fluids on the barn floor.

Ann also told police that Dee had hired Wayne Tidwell's backhoe service to dig and cover a massive pit. When police questioned Wayne Tidwell, he said he did indeed dig the pit and mentioned the horrible smell when he returned to cover it up.

That April, detectives asked the new property owner if he had purchased the property from Art Venecia and the man said he had. However, when they showed him a photo of Art he said that it wasn't him. Instead, he told detectives that he'd bought the property from was much younger man.

Later that day, police began digging in the trash pit. By nightfall they found the bodies of Art Venecia and his mother, Bessie Fischer.

———

Dee Casteel was shocked when she was arrested. In her mind, she was innocent. She hadn't killed anyone. She had made arrangements in almost every step of the two murders and committed fraud but claimed that she had no idea any of it was a crime.

Alan Bryant, Mike Irvine, William Rhodes, and Dee Casteel were each charged with two counts of first-degree murder, burglary, armed robbery, and grand theft.

During the trial, several witnesses testified that Dee, Mike, and Bil were otherwise good, likable people. However, even those friends of Alan Bryant that testified on his behalf said he was a habitual liar and a sociopath.

In September 1987, all four were found guilty and sentenced to death in the electric chair. In 1990, however, their convictions were overturned and their sentences were commuted to life in prison.

Years later, in interviews, Dee Casteel admitted that prison was good for her. She was finally able to put her alcohol problems behind her. She died in prison in 2002 at the age of sixty-four.

CHAPTER 8
THE BUSHY-HAIRED STRANGER

Vicki Lynne Hoskinson was born on February 2, 1976: Groundhog Day. As she was learning to speak, however, she couldn't quite pronounce the word groundhog and, even as an eight-year-old, she jokingly called it "Hound Dog Day."

Vicki loved Barbie dolls, playing softball, and eating her mother's tacos – but most of all, she loved the shiny, new, pink bicycle she got for Christmas.

On the afternoon of September 17, 1984, Vicky had just arrived home from Homer Davis Elementary School in Tucson, Arizona, where she had recently started third grade. She was excited to go out riding her bike. She was usually only allowed to ride with her sister, Stephanie, but her older sister was still at school.

Vicki begged her mother, Debbie Carlson, to let her ride her bike and, after persistent requests, Debbie told Vicki she could run an errand. She could ride two blocks away to the

Circle K convenience store to mail a birthday card to her aunt.

Vicki was excited. She cut through the dirt path behind her home and down to a dead-end street, then through an undeveloped lot of desert brush to get to the mailbox. She dropped the letter in the mailbox and started the journey home, but Vicki never returned. She had vanished.

————

The trip to the mailbox should have only taken ten minutes, but when twenty minutes passed her mother noticed she hadn't returned. Debbie thought that she might have stopped off at a friend's house on the way home. However, Vicki's sister Stephanie had just returned home from school and Debbie tasked the older daughter with going out to find Vicki.

It only took a few minutes before Stephanie ran home. Out of breath, it was clear the young girl was hysterical. "Her bike is lying in the middle of the road!" she screamed to her mother.

Debbie and Stephanie drove to the scene and, just as Stephanie had said, Vicki's bike laid in the middle of the road just a few blocks from their home. There was no sign of Vicki.

Debbie put the bicycle in the trunk of her car and drove through the neighborhood looking for her daughter while Stephanie frantically knocked on nearby friends' doors. But Debbie knew she wasn't just visiting a friend. Vicki loved that bicycle and she never would have left it lying in the street. Debbie knew there was something terribly wrong and called 911.

———

By evening, hundreds of police, fire crew, Sheriff's deputies, and members of the public were diligently looking for eight-year-old Vicki. For days, helicopters hovered over the neighborhood of Flowing Wells as friends and family members passed out fliers on the streets and in shops.

The missing girl was front page news and television stations ran updates on the case every few hours as tips came in. After two days, the FBI was called in to assist with the case of the missing girl.

The first glimmer of hope came from a woman that worked at the nearby Tucson Mall. The woman told police that she had seen a young girl who matched Vicki's description with an adult woman. She said the young girl was noticeably upset and kept begging to go home. The woman accompanying the girl tried buying her a toy to appease her but she was still upset. The mall employee worked with FBI sketch artists and a composite drawing was released to the public. Still, detectives had their doubts that someone would kidnap a young girl and then take her to a busy public mall.

———

Police spoke to children in the neighborhood that had seen Vicki riding her bike that afternoon. Two young boys told police that they were riding their bicycles in the opposite direction as Vicki as she was riding towards her home when they noticed a small black sports car driving slowly through the neighborhood. They also noticed that it had California license plates.

The mother of a three-year-old boy brought her son to the police to tell his story. Vicki's bicycle had been found in the street directly in front of their home and, although he was young, the boy had seen the abduction occur. The boy had been playing in the front yard that afternoon when he saw what he described as a "black race car" hit Vicki on her bicycle. He told police that a "big woman with long hair" got out of the car and helped the girl up, then they drove off together.

———

FBI agents revisited the scene where Vicki's bicycle had been found and noticed that a nearby mailbox had been damaged. The metal pole that held the mailbox had a fresh bend about twelve inches from the ground. It seemed that a car may have backed into the mailbox recently. The bend being so close to the ground indicated it could have been created by a sports car. This supported the description of the three-year-old and the two boys who had seen Vicki. Police were now looking for a dark-colored sports car that was low to the ground and possibly had California plates.

———

The most important tip, however, came from a coach at the nearby Homer Davis Elementary School. Sam Hall had supervised students that afternoon as they played in the schoolyard, when a little girl told him that a man had made obscene gestures to her from his car.

Hall then saw a black Datsun 280-Z driving slowly near the school. The man driving the car had long, messy black hair and a beard. He noticed that the man seemed upset, gestured strangely, and struggled with the car's stick shift. What troubled Hall most, however, was how creepily the man stared at the children as they played.

Hall had the foresight to memorize the car's license plate number, wrote it down, and called the police.

———

When police ran the California license plate number of the Datsun 280-Z, they found it was registered to twenty-eight-year-old Frank Jarvis Atwood. Moreover, the address on the registration was in Brentwood – the most affluent neighborhood of Los Angeles, with hundreds of million-dollar homes.

Frank Atwood's police record dated back to his teen years. His juvenile record included an arrest at sixteen for "sexual perversion," for which he was only counseled and released. His adult record had convictions for both kidnapping and child molestation.

When Vicki Lynne Hoskinson went missing, Atwood had been recently released from prison. He was out on parole for abusing an eight-year-old boy in a case where he had forced the boy off his bicycle, pulled him onto his motorcycle, and raped him.

Atwood had plea-bargained the child molestation charge down to abduction and was sentenced to five years in prison. He was released after serving only three years.

Detectives traveled to the Los Angeles address listed on the car's registration. The home belonged to Atwood's parents. His father, a retired Army Brigadier General and president of a large cable television company, admitted that their son had had many prior run-ins with the law. Atwood's father cooperated with the detectives and told them that Frank had been at their home a few days prior, but they didn't know where he was now. Atwood's mother, however, was much more protective of her son and reluctant to give detectives much information.

However, just hours after detectives left the Atwood home, Frank called his parents and spoke to his mother. He was in Kerrville, Texas, and his Datsun 280-Z had broken down. The car needed a new transmission and his mother was eager to help. Mrs. Atwood wrote down the mechanic's address and told her son that she would wire him money immediately so he could get the car fixed.

Frank's father, however, felt for the missing girl's family and knew the right thing to do. So, he copied the address in Texas, went to a pay phone so his wife wouldn't interfere, and called the FBI.

———

Four days after Vicki went missing, Frank Atwood was detained in Kerrville, Texas, along with James McDonald, a friend that had been traveling with him. But there was no sign of Vicki Lynne Hoskinson.

When investigators impounded his Datsun 280-Z and examined the front bumper, they found a small line of pink paint that they believed had been transferred from Vicki's bicycle. There was also damage to the gravel pan beneath the front of the car.

During questioning, Atwood admitted that he had been in the same Tucson neighborhood when Vicki went missing but insisted he had nothing to do with her disappearance. He had been temporarily living in the park near the school, as did several other homeless people.

Atwood told detectives he had left the park at 3:00 that afternoon to buy drugs and returned around 5:00 p.m., but he had no explanation for his whereabouts during the two-hour window.

His friend, James McDonald, gave the same story but with some extra detail. McDonald explained that he and Atwood had been arguing at 3:00 when Atwood left. He claimed that when Atwood returned two hours later, his hands, clothes, boots, and a knife were covered with blood and he had cactus needles stuck in his hands.

When McDonald asked what happened, Atwood told him that he'd gotten into a fight with a man he was trying to buy drugs from and had stabbed him. McDonald told police that two other men living in a trailer in the same park could verify the story. Police in Tucson followed up with the two other men, who gave the same account of events.

Frank Atwood was charged with one count of kidnapping and extradited from Texas back to Arizona. At his arraignment in December 1984, he pleaded not guilty.

————

Vicki's family and thousands of volunteers in the Tucson area were still desperately searching for the little royal-blue-eyed eight-year-old. Unfortunately, their suspect had a history of kidnapping and child molestation. As a result, their hopes of finding her alive were waning.

Yellow ribbons were tied all over the city and protesters took to the streets to vent their anger against lenient laws that allowed convicted child molesters back on the streets.

The people of Tucson were livid and rage spread through the community. Even though Atwood didn't live in Tucson, a protester set fire to a house mistakenly believed to be his home.

———

Almost seven months after Vicki went missing, a hiker came across a tiny human skull in the Sonoran Desert. The pieces of skeleton had been scattered by animals. Over five days, investigators performed a grid search of twenty square miles of desert, searching for her remains. The advanced state of decomposition prevented the determination of a cause of death or if she had been sexually assaulted. Police did, however, use a lower jawbone with teeth attached to match the dental records of Vicki Lynne Hoskinson.

Traces of adipocere found on the skull helped investigators to determine an approximate cause of death. Adipocere, also known as mortuary wax, is a gray waxy substance that forms when a body experiences three distinct conditions; high temperature, bacteria, and water.

The area of desert where Vicki's body was found had not received rain since just a few days after she went missing. It hadn't rained during the next seven months. The presence of adipocere meant that her body had to have been present in the desert during those rainstorms just a few days after she went missing.

On May 30, 1985, Vicki was laid to rest in Tucson and murder was added to Frank Atwood's charges.

———

Because of the massive publicity the case garnered, the trial was moved to Phoenix and began in January 1987. Jury selection took six weeks and the entire trial was broadcast live on television.

Although there was no physical evidence that Vicki had been in Atwood's car, the prosecution presented paint transfer evidence. They showed that the paint from Vicki's bicycle had transferred to his bumper and the nickel from his bumper had transferred to her bicycle.

The paint samples taken from the bumper of Atwood's car were forensically examined and determined to be an exact match to the paint from her bicycle.

They also presented evidence that the pedal from Vicki's bicycle damaged the gravel pan of Atwood's vehicle. In addition, the damage to the mailbox on the road where her bicycle was found was at the same height as the rear bumper of his Datsun 280-Z.

Frank Atwood consistently maintained that he had nothing to do with Vicki's disappearance or murder and suggested that police and the FBI planted and fabricated evidence against him.

On March 26, 1987, Frank Jarvis Atwood was convicted of first-degree murder and on May 8, 1987, he was sentenced to death.

———

While on death row, Atwood got married, was baptized in the Greek Orthodox Christian church, earned two associate degrees, a bachelor's degree in English and pre-law, and a master's degree in literature. He wrote six books, five of which were published, as well as commissioned someone outside the prison to construct a website.

Both the website and his books went to great lengths to attempt an explanation of his innocence. He wrote that, in 1970 at the age of fourteen, he was kidnapped and sexually assaulted which left him with Post Traumatic Stress Disorder. By his mid-teens he was selling sexual favors to older men. By his late teens he became fully immersed in rock music, Eastern philosophies, drugs, anti-establishment activities, and sexual perversion.

Atwood claimed that, after his arrest in Texas, the FBI took the bumper off his vehicle and sent it to Arizona, where Vicki's bicycle was held. He suggested that detectives rubbed the pink paint onto the bumper. He claimed they then flew the bumper back to Texas and put it back on the car.

His "proof" was the photos of the bumper, where he claimed two men could be seen in the reflection of the bumper holding the bicycle.

He suggested that the police didn't follow up on the sighting of the woman at the Tucson Mall, who he believed may have been the real killer.

———

By April 2021, Frank Atwood had exhausted his appeals and, on June 8, 2022, he was put to death by lethal injection – more than thirty-seven years after Vicki's death.

Vicki's mother, Debbie Carlson, worked diligently to fight for victims' rights. She helped the state of Arizona establish its Amber Alert system in 2000.

CHAPTER 9
THEY GOT IN THE WAY

Louise Porton had been an angry girl for as long as her relatives could remember. At family get-togethers near Birmingham, England, she refused to socialize with the other children. Although the family was closely connected, meeting every Sunday afternoon at her grandmother's house, Louise always felt like an outsider. She would stand alone, away from her cousins, and watch them play from a distance. Not interacting. If the other children tried to speak with her, she'd snap, "Stay away from me, or I'll smash your face."

At an early age, even her mother and grandmother knew something about Louise wasn't quite right.

When Louise was eleven years old in 2007, her mother, Sharon, divorced her father and left Louise and her siblings to be raised by him. The event hit her hard and the young girl resented her mother for leaving the family. From that point forward, Louise did her best to avoid contact with her mother.

As Louise grew into her early teens, her grandmother gradually noticed that items from her house had disappeared. A piece of jewelry here, a bit of money there. She knew it had to be Louise – but when her grandmother confronted her about it, Louise snarled, "If you accuse me of this, I'll never come back to visit you again." Her grandmother knew Louise meant it. Not wanting to lose contact with her granddaughter, she just held her tongue when things went missing.

Louise had discovered sex by her mid-teens. More importantly, she discovered what she could get by using her sexuality. She realized that boys (and men) would do almost anything for sex. For something as simple as oral sex, they would gladly part with the one thing she valued most in the world – money.

By age eighteen, Louise openly accepted money and gifts for sex. She even bragged on her Facebook page about how much money she could make by selling sex.

Her behavior put her even more at odds with her family members, who had begun distancing themselves from her. Though her family warned her that her obsession had developed into a sex addiction, she ignored them and pushed herself further from her family.

In October 2014, eighteen-year-old Louise gave birth to her first daughter, Lexi. Two years later, in September 2016, she gave birth to her second daughter, Scarlett. Despite her sexual promiscuity the two girls had the same father, Chris Draper, although Louise and Chris were never in a committed relationship.

Although the girls were biologically his, Louise denied it. She did everything possible to convince Chris that the girls weren't his. From the moment Scarlett was born, Louise refused to let Chris see his youngest daughter. She named her Scarlett Vaughn to make him think that the girl wasn't his child and moved forty miles away, to Rugby, UK, to avoid contact with him. To this day, it's unclear what motivation Louise had in keeping the girls from their biological father.

Several times Chris had applied for custody or, at the very least, visitation rights with the girls, but his attempts were never successful.

In Rugby, Louise and her two young girls rented a flat from a friend of her mother's named Leigh-Anne Bradley. When she moved into the flat, however, Louise pawned her children off with Leigh-Anne at every chance she got. She was too busy meeting up with men she had met online. Her sex life was much more important to her. Seeing how Louise treated the two girls, Leigh-Anne was more than happy to watch them, partly to give them a respite from their angry mother. It was common for Louise to curse at the kids, telling them, "Shut the fuck up, or I'll give you something to cry about!"

Leigh-Anne once saw Louise grow frustrated with Lexi while she was having a temper tantrum. Louise picked the girl up off the floor by the wrist and screamed, "Get the fuck off the floor!" In yet another instance, as baby Scarlett crawled toward the back door, Louise grabbed her ankle and violently yanked her away from the door while Leigh-Anne watched in horror.

Louise was paid to meet with men almost every night of the week. Leigh-Anne babysat as many as four times a week and other neighbors watched them on the additional nights. Louise was without the children more than she was with them. Clearly, the children were a burden to the young mother's lifestyle.

———

Louise's grandmother, Joy, had always been the center of their tight-knit family. When she became terminally ill in early 2016, however, Louise refused to visit her in the hospital. The tension that her actions created within the family was palpable. By April, Joy had only hours to live and Louise was informed that it would be the last time she could make amends with her grandmother. But Louise still refused to go.

After her grandmother's death, Louise also refused to attend the funeral. For almost every member of the family, that was the last straw. After that, all but a few family members cut all ties with her and never spoke to her again.

———

Louise Porton's obsession with making money from her sexuality grew and grew. She joined a website called Purple Port and used the nickname "Lollypop." Her profile listed that she specialized in glamour, cosplay, and erotic photography. Although the site was a modeling site, she used it to sell sex. Her website profile description read:

 "I'm an easy person to get along with and reliable. I've modeled for about 2 years now. I work for pay or trade, depending on the assignment :)

I'm open to all types of photoshoots, so just ask me, and you never know. I may say yes.

If you wish to see pictures from photoshoots that aren't on my profile, please ask."

Louise joined several other dating sites, such as MeetMe and Badoo, intending to lure money from men for sex.

———

Eventually, due to an inevitable falling out with Leigh-Anne, Louise moved into temporary housing near her sister, Karen – one of the only relatives still speaking to her. Although Karen and Louise got along, Karen openly prodded her about her lifestyle choices. It was obvious to her sister that Louise was working as an escort and she only masqueraded her sex work as "modeling." Karen was also concerned that the children took a backseat to her carefree lifestyle.

Louise was open and honest to her sister about her sex work, even admitting that she had once left the children alone in the house while she had sex with a man outside in his van. Although Karen expressed her concern, Louise jokingly replied, "Don't worry, I'm gonna start giving them sleeping tablets."

What Karen didn't know was that this wasn't the only occasion that her sex work had intertwined with the children's life. Louise had also had sex with men in her home with her children present, telling the men, "We can do it as long as you're quiet."

———

On January 2, 2018, Louise spent the first half of the day communicating with several men she had met online. The messages were mostly about sex for money; however, she had mentioned to some men that her daughter, Lexi, was sick.

Later in the day, Louise messaged her sister, Karen, to tell her that Lexi had had some sort of fit. A seizure of some sort. Karen immediately told her to call for an ambulance, but Louise explained that she had already called 111, the non-emergency number for National Health Services in the UK. She said she was waiting for a callback.

The truth was, however, that Louise hadn't made the call. She didn't call 111 until eleven minutes after the message to her sister.

When Louise explained to the operator that Lexi had had a seizure and stopped breathing while watching television, the operator advised sending an ambulance to her apartment immediately. Louise, however, said that her father had just arrived and he could drive them to the hospital.

As her father rushed them to the hospital, Louise seemed to have little concern for her daughter. Her mind was some-where else. She messaged a man that she had met online and informed him how much she charged for sexual photos of her.

As doctors examined Lexi, Louise messaged another man. She wanted him to know that her services were always paid with cash upfront.

Just after 6:00 the next morning, Lexi was discharged from the hospital. Doctors were unable to find anything wrong with the girl and had no idea why she would have had a seizure.

In the early hours of January 4, Louise had been searching online for information about children's health and seizures. Later that day, CCTV cameras showed her going to another apartment in the building for forty minutes, leaving the children alone. Shortly after she returned to her apartment, she called 999 – the UK's emergency phone number.

When paramedics arrived, Lexi's fingers, eyes, and ears were tinged blue. She wasn't breathing but emergency crews were able to revive her and rushed her to the hospital.

As Louise sat with the paramedics in the back of the ambulance, they noticed she didn't seem to be upset at all. Instead, during the entire drive she never once reached over to touch her child. The paramedics noticed it was odd behavior for a mother.

After several hours of doctors looking over Lexi's condition, they were still unsure what could have caused her loss of breath. Their only possible explanation was either a lower respiratory tract infection or influenza.

Again in the hospital, while Lexi cried frantically, Louise didn't seem concerned. She barely noticed her daughter's suffering and hospital staff had to prompt her to comfort Lexi.

Lexi remained in the hospital for four days while doctors monitored her condition. During the stay, Louise snuck off to the hospital bathroom to take topless photos of herself. She sent the photos to several men on her favorite dating sites, telling one man that she would perform any kind of sex he wanted for £300. She also befriended a hospital security guard. The two exchanged eighty-seven text messages before agreeing on a price for sex.

On January 8, Lexi was discharged again from the hospital. Again, she was given a clean bill of health and doctors still couldn't find anything in particular wrong with her.

When they got home, Louise typed a search into Google – "can you actually die if blocks nose and forcibly closed mouth with tape?" She also read an article entitled "Man commits suicide by supergluing mouth shut."

––––––

Almost a week after Lexi's release from the hospital, Louise and the girls spent the day with Karen. As the girls played, Karen noticed they seemed happy, healthy, and rambunctious.

Louise and the girls returned home at 6:00 p.m. on January 14. CCTV cameras showed Lexi running excitedly toward the apartment door, active and energetic.

Four hours later however, at 10:00 p.m., Louise messaged a man online:

> Having tuff time with my 3yr old being ill from that deadly flu. Doctor's telling me she gonna die.

Moments later, she did a few more Google searches:

"Is it true you shit yourself when you die?"

"How long after drowning can someone be resuscitated?"

"How long does it take a body to go cold up to the shoulder?"

She then read an article with the headline, "5 weird things that happen after you die." Another article read, "Toddler brought back to life after nearly drowning."

Just after midnight, Louise called 999 and told the operator that Lexi had stopped breathing.

When paramedics arrived twelve minutes later, Lexi's skin was pale with tiny brown spots. Her lips were blue and her jaw was stiff. Rigor mortis had already set in, which meant Lexi had been dead for a minimum of two hours before Louise had called for an ambulance.

Medical examiners took various samples from Lexi for a postmortem examination but doctors found no signs of foul play. The cause of death was not natural but they also failed to notice anything suspicious about it. At the time, the death of Lexi Draper was not treated as a homicide.

By the end of the day – the same day that her daughter died – Louise Porton was back to chatting with men online. She reached out to strangers for sympathy and mentioned to one man that her daughter had died.

> It's only me and this one now. I had 2. Now I'm down to 1.

She spent that evening uploading more photos of herself to apps and modeling sites, then made a post on Facebook:

> "RIP, my sleeping angel. We'll never forget you. Mommy loves you. Can't believe you're gone."

The following day, January 16, Louise accepted forty-one friend requests on her MeetMe app. She messaged one of the men and mentioned her daughter passing away the previous day. However, she still agreed to meet with him, as long as she could get her sister to watch Scarlett.

Two days after Lexi's death Karen confronted her sister and told her she was acting strangely – as if nothing was wrong. She was emotionless. Louise, however, told her sister that it was her way of coping. She was just trying to be strong for Scarlett.

Only nine days had passed when Louise mentioned something odd to a man online while talking about her daughter's death. She wrote,

> I hope Scarlett doesn't go the same way.

———

On February 1, Louise told her sister that she couldn't stand the memory of Lexi at her apartment anymore. She and Scarlett left the apartment and checked into a nearby hotel for the night.

Louise spent the hours between 7:00 and 10:00 p.m. chatting with several men online, some of which she expressed concern to about losing another daughter.

> Any chance of putting £30 in my bank account now for fuel to get my daughter Scarlett to the hospital? She's not well. I'm not losing another baby

The man quickly replied:

> Call the ambulance. Don't waste any time.

She told the man that she had already called 999 and they had told her to just drive to the hospital. Louise continued asking men for money to fill her gas tank, promising she would pay it back.

Thirteen minutes later, she messaged another man:

> Taking Scarlett to the hospital in a bit. She ain't well. She's had flu-like me. I need your support. If Scarlett goes bad, I can't deal with this alone again.

Another twelve minutes passed before Louise left the hotel with Scarlett in her arms. The girl was already cold and motionless. As she left the hotel lobby, she mentioned to the hotel staff that her daughter was only sleeping.

As Louise Porton drove toward the hospital, she stopped to fill up her tank, then stopped again at a retail shopping center. Thirty minutes after leaving her hotel room, she pulled over in an empty parking lot and called 111 – the non-emergency number. She explained to the operator that her daughter was sleeping in the car, but she wanted to make sure she didn't pass away as her other daughter had done two weeks earlier. The operator told her to check for vital signs but there were none.

When emergency crews arrived at 10:30 that evening, Scarlett lay on the front passenger seat of the car with her eyes closed, not breathing. Ambulance crews noted that the seventeen-month-old girl was freezing and completely lifeless.

When Scarlett arrived at the hospital, doctors discovered that she had been starved of oxygen and dead for a very long time. Scarlett was already dead when her mother was begging for money from men online.

In situations like this, it was standard procedure for a hospital to assign a nurse to watch over a grieving parent after losing a child. However, the nurse assigned to comfort Louise noticed that she wasn't reacting to the death in the way a typical parent would have. There were no tears or crying. Instead, she simply scrolled through her phone, even showing the nurse photos of tattoos she wanted to get.

———

Only two weeks had passed between the two deaths of her children. It was more than suspicious circumstances and a police investigation was launched. Forensic experts were called to conduct extensive examinations of both girls and the situations leading up to their deaths.

Upon closer examination, however, they found that both girls had died of deliberate airway obstruction. Tiny marks on Lexi's face indicated that her nose had been pinched or pinned shut for an extended period of time.

Bruising on the soft tissue of Scarlett's neck was even more telling. When police searched the hotel room where Louise and Scarlett had been staying, they found tiny spots of Scarlett's blood on her pillow.

———

Three days after Scarlett's death, Louise met with the housing office to find a new place to live. The worker handling her case noted that Louise seemed emotionless. "It was almost like someone who had lost their goldfish."

Louise Porton was initially arrested on March 20, 2018, but prosecutors simply didn't have enough evidence to charge her with murder and she was released. It would take almost another year for investigators to gather more evidence. Finally, on January 25, 2019, she was charged with the murders of her two children.

The double-murder trial began on July 3. Jurors read her many messages to men online just after the murders that showed behavior atypical to that of a grieving mother. The most damning of the messages were sent to a man named Kim, just before Scarlett's death:

Lexi died. Scarlett may go the same.

Louise was asked why she would have said that when Scarlett was perfectly healthy at the time. She had no answer, only claiming that she couldn't remember.

Paramedics that responded to her emergency calls testified about her lack of emotion after the murders. For example, one paramedic testified that he saw Louise a few weeks after Lexi's death while responding to another emergency. During the incident, she seemed happy to see him and introduced him to her friends, saying, "He's the medic that looked after my Lexi before she died."

Louise was questioned about the bruising to Scarlett's head and abrasions on her neck, but she had no explanation.

She pleaded,

 "Why would I kill my own kids? My children were never an inconvenience to me, and I accommodated my personal lifestyle around them.

It is correct that life as a single mother is difficult, but I never asked anyone for money, and any suggestion that I used my daughter's ill health or death to make money is wholly inaccurate and wrong. I never regretted having them. They were always giving me something to do, and I would take them to places like parks and give them a good life."

Louise Porton was found guilty of killing her daughters and received a life sentence with the possibility of parole in thirty-two years.

————

During the time before her arrest, Louise's mother, Sharon, reached out to her daughter and defended her against the accusations that she had killed Lexi and Scarlett. Because she supported her daughter, however, Sharon was harassed by many people who accused her of raising a killer. However, Louise and Sharon's rekindled relationship didn't last long.

Just before the trial, the two argued and Louise punched her mother in the face. Sharon realized that her daughter had indeed killed Lexi and Scarlett; Sharon was now tormented by the realization. She posted on Facebook about the incident and publicly disowned her daughter, calling her a monster.

 "Something snapped in her head. She became a monster, and my wonderful little girl changed. She's not the happy, loving girl I brought up. I no longer consider her my daughter."

Even after Louise's conviction, the public continued to harass Sharon and she fell into a deep depression. In February 2020, at just forty-eight years old, Sharon committed suicide.

Eighteen months after their deaths, Lexi and Scarlett's father, Chris Draper, gave the girls a proper burial with a funeral carriage pulled by four white horses draped in purple.

CHAPTER 10
THE CONMAN

Barrington, Rhode Island, was a small but affluent suburb situated just seven miles southeast of Providence, Rhode Island, and surrounded by waterways that eventually led to Narragansett Bay, then further south to the Atlantic Ocean.

The sleepy town of fifteen thousand was shocked in September 1991 when a local lawyer, Ernest Brendel, his wife, Alice, who worked as a librarian at Brown University in Providence, and their eight-year-old daughter, Emily, all disappeared without a trace.

Six weeks after their disappearance, the town of Barrington learned that they had been living with a sociopath in their midst.

———

Christopher Hightower was born in 1949 in Winterhaven, Florida. He was the eldest of five children but as he reached his teen years, he discovered that the man he had known as his father his entire life was not his biological father. His four siblings were only his half-siblings. Christopher's birth father had abandoned his mother when she became pregnant at seventeen.

The realization that his mother and stepfather had lied to him his entire life created angst that his parents couldn't control. He resented both of them, particularly his stepfather. When he was old enough to leave home, Christopher shunned his parents, joined the Navy, and never looked back.

His anger toward his parents drove his desire to make a name for himself. He wanted to be more than just a printer like his stepfather.

In 1973, after four years in the Navy, Christopher Hightower married and studied zoology at the University of Rhode Island. His true desire, however, was to go to medical school. He wanted to become a doctor.

The problem with that was that Hightower had never gotten particularly good grades. He was a solid C student. With grades like that, he could never qualify for medical school.

There was also the issue of money. Although Hightower and his wife owned a house, they had no money for him to attend such an expensive school. That didn't deter him, though. Hightower attempted to sell the family home to pay for his college tuition – but when his wife discovered what he was trying to do, the two divorced after seven years of marriage.

In 1982 Hightower met a new partner and married again. Still wanting to enroll in medical school, he applied for admission to Wright State University in Ohio. However, he knew he could never get approved with his current transcripts – so, to alleviate the problem, he paid someone to manipulate his transcripts. He was now a straight-A student.

During his brief time at Wright State University, Hightower became fascinated by the stock market and joined an investment group. The others in the group were impressed by his interest in stocks and commodities. Hightower's natural gift, however, was his ability to sell people his investment schemes.

Hightower managed to dupe his friends and colleagues out of almost $100,000 with get-rich-quick investment promises. However, he wasn't investing the money at all. Instead, he kept the money and left Ohio before being prosecuted.

Christopher Hightower and his wife, Susan, were now parents to two children and had moved back to Rhode Island, to the small town of Barrington. Susan's wealthy parents had a large home that was large enough for the entire family to live together.

Hightower and his family fit in well in the upscale suburb and he knew that if he applied himself, he could make his fortune as an investment broker to the wealthy inhabitants of Barrington.

Christopher Hightower opened a small investment office at 500 Maple Avenue and named it Hightower Investments, then applied for trading licenses with the National Futures Association and the Commodities Futures Trading Commission.

He and his family attended the Barrington Congressional Church, where he taught Sunday school. It was the perfect place to get clients for his investments. He also coached soccer at the local Junior High school and was active in the community. Before long, Hightower had several clients.

One client that Hightower became friends with was Ernest Brendel. Ernie and his wife, Alice, became good friends with the Hightower family. Their relationship was so close that Christopher Hightower was on the list of approved people allowed to pick up their eight-year-old daughter, Emily, after school.

Hightower had worked his magic on Ernie and promised him riches through investing in commodity futures. Ernie fell for it hook, line, and sinker. He took fifteen thousand dollars from his retirement fund and entrusted Hightower to make it into much, much more. Hightower, however, knew it would never work.

Over the course of the following year, Ernie Brendel watched the balance of his investment account dwindle further and further toward zero. Eventually, when the account was down to only three thousand dollars, Ernie had had enough. He confronted Hightower but it was no use talking to him. He had an excuse for everything. Left with no choice, Ernie wrote a letter to the Commodities and Futures Trading Commission demanding that Hightower's trading licenses be revoked.

By that time, Christopher Hightower had been pilfering money from people all over town but his financial woes weren't his only problems. His wife, Susan, had had enough and had petitioned for a divorce. Without his wife, Hightower would be on the street. He could no longer live in the fancy house or lead the luxurious lifestyle that her parents provided for them. Ernie Brendel's letter was going to put an end to his ability to scam any more clients.

Hightower saw no other option than to threaten his wife. He knew that he would probably never see his children again if they divorced. He told her he had paid a hitman $5,000 to kill her. He said he'd even paid an extra $1,000 to hide the body so she would never be found. All she had to do was call off the divorce and he would call off the killer.

As for fifty-three-year-old Ernie Brendel, Hightower devised a plan. For days, he watched the family come and go from their home and learned their daily routines.

On Thursday, September 19, 1991, Hightower drove six miles north to a sporting goods store in Seekonk, Massachusetts. He purchased a high-power Bear Devastator crossbow, six crossbow bolts, and six special bullet-point tips before he returned to Barrington.

Hightower parked near the Brendel home and watched as Emily boarded the school bus outside their home, then watched as Ernie drove Alice to work in Providence. While they were away, he broke into the house and waited patiently in the garage with the crossbow.

When Ernie Brendel returned home and entered the garage, he didn't stand a chance. Hightower shot him with the crossbow in the chest, then again in the buttocks. It was the third shot that killed him. It went through his back, piercing his spinal cord, then continued through his esophagus before it punctured his heart. However, Hightower still wanted to make sure he was dead. He grabbed a nearby crowbar and beat him about the head, fracturing his skull.

Christopher Hightower spent the rest of the morning scrubbing the garage floor with hydrochloric acid and doing his best to eliminate any signs of a crime. He piled Ernie Brendel's body into the trunk of Alice's Toyota and drove to the edge of town, where he had already dug a shallow grave. He buried Ernie's body and sprinkled lime on the ground to mask the smell of decomposition.

Hightower went home, took a shower, and washed his clothes – but just as he finished, he realized the Sheriff was waiting for him at his front door. The Sheriff, however, had no idea that he had just murdered a man. Instead, he was there to serve him with a restraining order. The restraining order stipulated that Hightower could no longer be anywhere near his wife, nor could he live in her parents' house.

With nowhere to go, Hightower returned to the Brendel home, where he sat in their living room, listened to messages on their answering machine, and planned the remainder of his day.

Hightower called Emily's school pretending to be Ernie and told them it was okay for the young girl to walk home from school that day. School staff, however, said there was no way they would agree to that. That was against school policy and it wouldn't be allowed.

He then drove Alice's car to the local YMCA, where he knew that Emily was involved in after-school activities. He told the staff that he was there to pick her up, but he didn't know that Ernie had already removed him from the list of approved people.

Undeterred, he went to a payphone and called the YMCA, again posing as Ernie Brendel. He told them it was okay for Christopher Hightower to pick up his daughter and, to prove it, he would be carrying Ernie's driver's license.

Emily knew something was wrong. She knew how upset her father was with Hightower and that he wouldn't have allowed him to pick her up. Emily insisted that the YMCA staff call her home and speak to her father but, when her father didn't answer, she left a message on the answering machine, "Dad, Dad! This doesn't seem right!"

The ploy worked despite Emily's complaints. Hightower showed Ernie Brendel's driver's license to the YMCA staff and took her back to the Brendel home. Once in the house, he fed her a hefty dose of Benadryl to make her drowsy and tied her arms and legs with telephone cords.

Alice typically took the bus home from work and Ernie would pick her up at the bus stop, but today he wasn't there and she walked home. Hightower attacked and subdued her inside her home when she walked through the front door.

He seated Alice in front of the family computer and forced her to type. He wanted her to pen a letter as her husband, Ernie, to the Commodities and Futures Trading Commission stating that he was mistaken about Christopher Hightower and wished to withdraw his complaint against him. Alice typed as Hightower loomed over her shoulder. When she finished typing, he grabbed a sheet of Ernie's business letterhead and printed it, then had her forge Ernie's name.

With the letter in hand, he no longer had a use for Alice and Emily. Hightower took one of Alice's scarves, wound it around her neck, and twisted the life out of her. He then piled Alice and the sleeping Emily into the trunk of her Toyota before he again drove to the edge of town. Just next to where he buried Ernie, he dug another shallow grave. He threw Emily in first – face-down, sleeping but still alive. He then threw her mother on top of the girl and filled the hole. Again, he sprinkled lime around the area to hide the smell.

———

The following day Christopher Hightower drove Alice's bloody car around town as if nothing had happened. He used Ernie's checkbook to write checks for gasoline, cleaning supplies, and frozen yogurt.

On September 22, he drove ninety-five miles south to Guilford, Connecticut, to the home of Ernie's sister, Christine Scriabine. Christine had never met Christopher Hightower and had no idea that Ernie and his family were missing.

Hightower told Christine that the mafia had kidnapped the entire Brendel family. Then, to make it look legitimate, he told her they had also kidnapped his own family. To further prove his point, he showed Ernie's bank cards, his driver's license, some of Ernie's personal documents, and several rings that belonged to Alice.

According to Hightower, the mafia demanded $300,000 for the safe return of both families. He said he could cover $175,000 of the ransom himself and $50,000 from Ernie's brokerage account but he asked that Christine and her husband come up with the final $75,000.

He told Christine and her husband that the men who had kidnapped them broke Ernie's jaw as they were trying to take him away, then he showed them the trunk of Alice's Toyota. Inside they saw an enormous amount of blood. Christine's husband was a physician and knew that a blood stain like that had to have come from much more than a broken jaw. If a person had lost that much blood, they wouldn't have survived.

It was quite a story and Christine wasn't sure she could believe what the stranger was telling her. Besides, she didn't have $75,000 lying around the house. Before he left, Hightower told them that the mafia had made it clear that the families would be killed if there was any police involvement. He also said he knew that they'd tapped their phone.

When Hightower finally left at 1:00 a.m., they went to a neighbor's house and called the FBI.

When the Barrington police broke into the Brendel residence, they initially didn't notice any signs of a struggle. However, as they searched they noticed that telephone cords were missing and someone had broken a window to the garage.

On September 23, police took Christopher Hightower into custody as he left a shopping center driving Alice's car. Hightower maintained the same story he told Christine – that the mafia had kidnapped the Brendel family and demanded a ransom, but police didn't believe him for a minute.

Inside the car was an ungodly amount of dried blood. It was far more blood than a broken jaw would produce. Investigators found three adult teeth that were later matched to Ernie's dental records. There was also an empty bag of lime and a crossbow bolt in the trunk.

Detectives questioned Hightower until the early hours of the following morning. When one detective stood up to leave, he told Hightower that he was going to Hightower's home to look at tire tracks. But, as the detective walked through the door, Hightower made a fatal mistake. He blurted out, "Sarge, you're wasting your time. They're not buried there."

For the next several months, multiple branches of law enforcement and volunteers searched for the bodies of the Brendel family – it was obvious they were dead. Meanwhile, forensic investigators found a small hole in the garage door that matched the crossbow bolt located in the trunk of Alice's car. They also found blood spatter throughout the garage.

On October 2, the National Futures Association and the Commodities Futures Trading Commission informed the FBI that they had received a letter supposedly from Ernie Brendel asking to have his complaint withdrawn. The letter had been postmarked three days after the Brendel family was already missing. After careful examination of the letter, forensic document examiners determined it to be a forgery. Investigators had also found a file containing the letter on the Brendel home computer. Alice seemed to have left a clue when she named the file using Christopher Hightower's initials.

————

On November 7, 1991, six weeks after the Brendel family had gone missing, Katherine McCloy was walking her dogs through a wooded area behind the St. Andrew's School in Barrington. One of the dogs, however, wouldn't come back when called. When she got to a clearing, she walked through thick bushes to look for the dog. The dog was sniffing in a small area in the clearing where she could clearly see two large indentations in the soil. She noticed a white, powdery substance covering the indentations. Katherine was an avid gardener and she suspected the powder was lime, so she walked home and called the police.

Ernie's body was found in the first grave with two crossbow bolt holes in his chest and one in his buttocks. His skull was fractured and he had several lacerations on his scalp. Alice and Emily were buried together in a separate grave next to Ernie. Alice had died of strangulation with her scarf still around her neck. Emily's cause of death was undetermined but medical examiners believed she had been buried alive. Near the top of the grave, investigators also found a torn corner of a bag of lime that matched the bag found in the trunk of Alice's Toyota.

Christopher Hightower was charged with three counts of murder, one count of kidnapping a child under sixteen, two counts of breaking and entering, forgery and counterfeiting, and unlawful burial.

At his trial, Hightower took the stand in his own defense despite his lawyer advising him against it. He attempted to sell the same old mafia story. He claimed that he had witnessed members of the mafia strangling eight-year-old Emily. He told the jury that the men put a pillowcase over his head, walked him into the woods, and forced him to dig the graves.

His wide, unblinking eyes gave him a crazed stare during his testimony. Finally, when his defense realized the mafia story wasn't working, they brought in a psychiatrist that testified Hightower was delusional.

The prosecution presented almost 100 witnesses, including an employee from the sporting goods store that sold him the crossbow and a delivery driver who spoke to Hightower at the Brendel home. Other witnesses included neighbors who saw him cleaning the garage after Ernie Brendel had gone missing.

Investigators had tracked Hightower through various receipts where he had paid for gasoline, cleaning supplies, and the acid he used to clean the garage floor. To further show what type of a person Hightower was, the prosecution confronted him about the school transcripts he falsified to get into school eleven years prior.

On June 8, 1993, Christopher Hightower was found guilty and sentenced to life in prison without the possibility of parole.

CHAPTER 11
THE SWINDLER

Chazz and Janine Sutphen had a long and happy marriage. She was a classically-trained cellist and the couple raised their three sons in a musical family in Vermont. But in 1994, when Chazz developed a heart condition and died, Janine's world changed. She went through bouts of depression but always pulled herself together.

By the late 1990s, her boys were full-grown and had moved away from home. Janine felt lonely. Determined to make herself happy, she packed her bags and moved to Durham, North Carolina, where she got a job playing cello with the Durham Symphony Orchestra. Music was her passion and being able to play professionally made her extremely happy.

Janine was active with the Unitarian Church. She first met Rob Petrick at a church summer camp in 1999. They were both in their fifties. Rob had no job but tinkered with Apple computers as a means of occasional money. He was divorced and had recently moved to Durham as well. The two started dating and it quickly grew into a whirlwind romance. Within a year, they were married. Janine's three sons were surprised that she remarried and a little worried that Rob may have been searching for a free ride, but as long as he made her happy, they were delighted. They seemed to be the perfect, happy couple for the next year and a half, often finishing each other's sentences.

Her sons, Christopher, Darren, and Robin Sutphen, called their mother regularly. A day usually wouldn't pass without one of them calling their mother. But in early January 2003, Janine fell ill. She had been sick for a few days and told her sons that she was feeling a bit depressed again too. She had always gotten through her depression in the past, so her sons weren't too concerned – but they began to worry when she stopped answering the phone on January 7.

The sons regularly called to check in on their mother but they usually got no answer. Finally, Rob occasionally answered and tried handing the phone to her, but he told her sons that she was in bed and just too depressed to talk.

Frustrated and worried about their mother, Christopher called Rob and expressed his concern. He told Rob he planned to drive to Durham to check on her. Shortly after that, at 3:30 in the morning on January 22, Rob called the police to report his wife missing.

Rob Petrick told police that Janine had left for the Durham Symphony for practice at 6:30 the night before, but she hadn't returned home yet. Police quickly sprang into action and found her car in the parking garage adjacent to the Durham Arts Council.

The car was unlocked with the keys inside. Her very expensive cello was in clear view in the back seat. If she had been robbed, the perpetrator would have taken the cello. No windows had been broken and nothing was out of place. It was as if she had just left the car there.

Police spoke to business owners, checked surveillance cameras, and spoke to parking attendants, but there were no clues as to where she may have gone.

————

As with any missing person report, detectives began by questioning the husband, Rob. According to Rob, they had a solid relationship and never spent a night apart in their entire marriage. He mentioned that she had struggled with depression but he wasn't quite sure where she would have gone. He told the investigators that their finances were in order, they never argued, and they were still very much in love.

Neighbors and friends told investigators that they hadn't seen or heard from Janine in at least a week.

Detectives called the sons to let them know their mother was missing. When they spoke to the sons, however, they mentioned that their mother had never parked in that parking garage in the past. In fact, she had complained to the Council staff that it was very dark and dangerous at night. She always made a point of parking in the brightly-lit parking lot across the street.

They, too, told investigators that their mother had struggled with depression but had always come out of it. She was a very strong-willed woman and they couldn't believe she would have just walked away from life or committed suicide.

————

When forensic investigators took a closer look at the car, one detail didn't make sense. Janine was very short – only about four feet eleven inches tall. The driver's-side seat, however, was pushed back for a driver that was much taller than that. Janine couldn't have been the last person to drive that car. With that one piece of evidence, detectives knew there was a good chance that Janine wasn't alive.

During the prior interview with Rob, he had mentioned that both he and Janine were paid well at their jobs and had no financial problems to speak of. However, when detectives checked with Janine's banks to see if her credit cards were being used, they found that someone had completely drained her accounts and her credit cards were maxed out and overdue.

Janine's son, Christopher, couldn't believe his mother had overdue credit cards. Her whole life, she had never missed a payment. Then he remembered something his mother had said. Christopher told investigators that, during a recent phone call with his mother, she had mentioned something about missing mail. She hadn't been getting the credit card statements in the mail.

Detectives spoke to the mail carrier who delivered to Janine and Rob's home. The carrier said that he knew Rob well – he came out to the mailbox almost every day to pick up the mail as soon as it was delivered.

It was clear to investigators that something was wrong; they suspected Rob had drained Janine's bank accounts and hidden the bills from her.

Detectives served a search warrant and searched Rob's home. Rob was agitated and intimidating as the detectives searched his computer room, where he had several computers and hard drives strewn around.

There was no sign of Janine's possible whereabouts in the home but they did find evidence of a crime. Rob had been forging checks and committing fraud.

Detectives arrested Rob Petrick on felony fraud charges and his computers and hard drives were taken into evidence to be analyzed. Forensic investigators found shocking Google search queries in the browsing history of his computers.

He had searched phrases relating to how to deal with rigor mortis, how long bodies would stay at the bottom of a lake, and had even searched the query, "Neck snap break hold." He had also bookmarked a page entitled "22 ways to kill a man with your bare hands."

A deeper investigation revealed searches for underwater topographical maps of twelve North Carolina lakes.

Cadaver dogs searched the home and picked up the scent of death in his car's trunk, bathroom tub, and bedroom.

––––––

Detectives knew he had murdered Janine but, without a body, they needed physical evidence. Prosecutors weren't going to risk trying him for murder based only on his Google searches. Rob Petrick was released on bail within days of his fraud arrest.

Investigators knew they had their man and that Janine was dead. They just needed a way to prove it, so they began digging into Rob Petrick's background. They learned of his sordid past through speaking to close friends, relatives, ex-wives, and ex-lovers.

———

Rob Petrick grew up in Chicago and, within months of his birth, his father left the family. Throughout his childhood, the family moved nearly every year and he went through several stepfathers.

Petrick attended Catholic school, was an altar boy for a brief time, and teachers claimed he had genius-level abilities. Still, he was severely bullied and dropped out of high school when he was just sixteen, then hitchhiked around the country.

By the early 1980s, he found trouble. He had been arrested for fraud. In 1982 he married a high school friend, April Vandam, but it wasn't long before he racked up debt on her credit cards and forced her to file for bankruptcy.

Throughout the early 1980s he had several convictions of fraud and forgery and spent 1983 through 1985 in an Illinois prison. When he was released, he got a job as a mail carrier but spent six months in a federal halfway house when he was convicted of throwing mail into a dumpster in 1988.

By 1992 he had separated from April and moved in with a couple, Keith and Phaedra Oorbeck. The eccentric couple practiced neo-paganism, polygamy, and considered themselves witches. In September 1995, Petrick, Keith, and Phaedra were married in a neo-pagan wedding and lived in a polyamorous relationship. Their love triangle lasted four years before Petrick moved to Greensboro, North Carolina, with another woman.

———

Investigators learned that in June 2001, Janine had received a phone call from Lisa Oorbeck, another wife of Keith

Oorbeck. Lisa, who was a stranger to Janine, called to warn her about Petrick. She knew that he was seeing another woman. She also told Janine of his fraud schemes and history of paganism. But according to Lisa, Janine dismissed her warnings, telling her that she didn't believe her and it was too late anyway.

Detectives suspected there were many more women that Petrick had swindled and decided to go public with their suspicions about him. Police spoke to the media and asked that they cover the story of Petrick's fraud charges and their possible connection to his wife's disappearance.

The media had syndicated the story nationwide through newspapers when Ann Johnston noticed it, hundreds of miles away in Atlanta, Georgia, and called the Durham prosecutor's office. The story she told shocked detectives.

Ann Johnston told police that she had dated Rob Petrick in high school and, over a year ago, had just rekindled her relationship with him. She knew he lived in Durham but had no idea he was married. Petrick told her he had been previously married but his wife had died of cancer. Over the past year, he flew to Atlanta several times a month to stay with her and they had picked up right where their relationship had left off. In fact, he had already proposed to her and they had plans to be married.

Ann Johnston was wealthy, as were her parents; police knew that Petrick had set his sights on her as his next target.

As the articles about Rob Petrick spread through the country, more women came forward with similar stories. A Greensboro woman said she dated Petrick until he drained her bank accounts and maxed out her son's credit cards. Another Durham woman said that Petrick flirted with her in a bar a few days before Janine Sutphen was reported missing and he'd told her that his wife had recently died of cancer.

Another woman told police that she had dated Petrick until she found out he was married. Yet another said that he had wiped her out financially; he had been intercepting her mail and hiding credit card bills that he had racked up in her name.

Detectives grew more and more sure that Rob Petrick had murdered his wife but, without a body, they still couldn't bring charges against him.

———

Four months after she had been reported missing, kayakers found a large green tarp wrapped in the shape of a human body floating in Falls Lake, east of Durham.

When police arrived, they found the object wrapped tightly with duct tape and thick, rusted chains connected to cinder blocks. Investigators unraveled several layers of green tarp and sleeping bags to find the bloated body of Janine Sutphen.

As soon as she was identified using dental records, Rob Petrick was arrested and charged with murder.

———

Rob Petrick put on a show for the media and jurors. He pleaded not guilty and showed only arrogance, no remorse.

Before his trial, prosecutors offered Petrick a plea bargain that would have allowed him to combine the murder charge with his multiple fraud charges. It was a sweetheart deal that would have ensured his release from prison in only fifteen years.

But Petrick's narcissism wouldn't allow him to plead guilty. He didn't believe prosecutors had enough evidence to convict him and declined the deal.

He also didn't believe his court-appointed lawyer had his best interests at heart and fired him, choosing to represent himself instead. Petrick believed he was smarter than everyone.

Acting as his own attorney, Petrick questioned witnesses, including his former fiancé Ann Johnston and Janine's best friend, Peg Lewis, to show that he had never shown violent tendencies toward his wife or Ann. He admitted that he was a philanderer and swindler but not a cold-blooded killer.

He went on to question the dog handler that had discovered cadaver scents in his car and bathroom, as well as crime scene technicians, in an attempt to prove that there was no physical evidence against him.

He argued that anyone, including Janine herself, could have made the damning Google searches. He went on to argue that there was no way he could have crammed Janine's body in the trunk of his tiny two-seater Mazda Miata. He tried everything he could think of but his efforts were futile. He was not as clever as he thought.

Ultimately, Petrick dug his own grave and, on November 29, 2005, after just two hours of deliberation, a jury found him guilty and he was convicted of first-degree murder. Rob Petrick was sentenced to life in prison without parole.

CHAPTER 12
PRETTY IN PINK

Roselenna Gunelson was just fourteen when she gave birth to her daughter, Monica Kay, in 1997. Monica never knew her biological father, but Roselenna's partner, Joshane Karlen, adopted the girl as his own daughter when she was just four years old. Although Roselenna and Joshane divorced when Monica was twelve, she maintained a close relationship with her adoptive father.

As Monica entered her high school years, she went through a period where she struggled with her identity. Boy or girl? She knew she wasn't actually a boy, but she never felt that she fit into the girl mold either.

As a compromise, she petitioned to have her name legally changed to Ezra McCandless. Ezra sounded more gender-neutral to her and she took the name McCandless from Chris McCandless, the subject of the book and film Into the Wild.

Growing up in the tiny town of Stanley, Wisconsin, was hard for Ezra. Upon graduating high school, she spent a brief time in college but dropped out after only a year. She then moved to Eau Claire, Wisconsin: a slightly larger city with a population of just under 70,000.

Ezra was an amateur artist. She loved painting, drawing, writing, and taking artistic photos of herself and nature. She even used her car, a 2003 silver Chevy Impala, as a creative canvas with her drawings covering the hood and roof of the car.

Like many young people in the city, eighteen-year-old Ezra loved spending her time at a local coffee shop, Racy D'Lenes Coffee Lounge. There, she met thirty-three-year-old Jason Mengel, a medic in the National Guard. Despite their fourteen-year age difference, the two fell in love and had moved in together within a month.

Several months later, however, Ezra found herself pregnant. Although the couple had briefly tossed around the thought of marriage, the truth was that neither was ready to have a baby. So on October 6, Ezra spent her birthday driving to Minneapolis to have an abortion.

Jason and Ezra spent a lot of time at Racy's Coffee Shop, both together and separately, so they had a friend in common that worked there – Alex Woodworth.

Alex worked as a barista at Racy's. He had graduated from the University of Wisconsin and occasionally worked as a substitute teacher. He planned to get his master's degree and become a philosophy teacher and those dreams intrigued Ezra. She and Alex both shared a love of philosophy, art, and photography.

By late October that year, Ezra had developed a relationship with Alex that had become more than platonic. It had become a sexual relationship that involved BDSM, although she hid her affair from her boyfriend, Jason Mengel.

In early February, Jason was called away for two weeks for National Guard duty. When he returned and met with Ezra, he knew something was wrong. He could sense it. Curiosity drove him to read the text messages on her phone, where he found that not only had she been sleeping with Alex Woodworth but she had also slept with Jason's best friend, John Hansen.

The texts to John Hansen showed that Ezra wasn't exactly the innocent girl Jason believed her to be. The texts read of bondage and domination.

When Jason confronted Ezra about the text messages, she denied having an affair with John. Instead, according to Ezra, John had raped her.

Jason was livid. He confronted his friend, John, who flatly denied raping her. Wanting to believe his girlfriend, Jason took Ezra to the police station to report the assault. Ezra explained to the police that she and John had been drinking, but she passed out after drinking too much. That was when John took advantage of her, she said.

Police investigated the incident and questioned others that had been there on the night of drinking, including Alex Woodworth. However, Alex had a different story to tell. He explained that he knew Ezra wasn't raped because Ezra had explicitly told him she had willingly had sex with John. She had told him that she felt guilty for cheating on Jason with two men, but it was 100% consensual sex. With this news, the district attorney refused to bring any charges against John and the case was dropped.

The ordeal, however, destroyed the relationship between Jason and Ezra. He no longer wanted anything to do with her, his friend John, or Alex Woodworth.

Ezra McCandless felt the world closing in on her. She knew she had made an irrevocable mistake and abused the trust of the one man she truly loved. So, she packed her bags and moved forty miles north back to Stanley, Wisconsin, to live with her mother.

From her mother's home, Ezra continued to try to patch things up with Jason. She pleaded with him that neither of the affairs were her fault. She explained that both Alex and John were manipulative men trying to steal her away from him. She told him she was willing to do anything to be with him. Anything. She had been writing about her horrible betrayal in journals and wanted Jason to read them but he refused. Although Jason's heart had been broken, there was no way he could trust her again. He told her they were done. It was over. Then he cut off all communication with her.

In Ezra's mind, her relationship with Jason had ended because of Alex Woodworth. If he had just kept his mouth shut when he spoke to the police, she and Jason might still be together. On February 24, she sent Alex an angry text message telling him to never talk to her again.

———

Almost a month had passed when Jason Mengel was surprised to see Ezra McCandless walk into Racy's Coffee Shop on the morning of March 22. Trying to maintain some civility, the two spoke briefly. He asked what she was doing in town but noticed she seemed nervous and flustered. Ezra said she had only come to town to return some things to a friend, but Jason felt something was wrong. She wasn't acting normally.

As Ezra drove away from the coffee shop, Jason began to worry. After thinking about the situation for a few minutes, Jason hopped on his bicycle and started riding toward Alex Woodworth's house.

When he arrived at the house, Ezra's Chevy Impala was idling in the driveway with the driver's side door open but there was no sign of her. Jason circled around on his bicycle for a while, then parked it outside the house. Nervous, he paced back and forth on the sidewalk, waiting for her to come out of the house. After waiting for forty-five minutes, he walked into the house without knocking to find Ezra and Alex calmly talking on the couch.

Jason could see that she was safe and he was a bit embarrassed to have walked in on them unannounced. He walked back outside to wait for her to finish her conversation, but as he left the house, a police car pulled up. A neighbor had noticed Jason's nervous pacing on the sidewalk and called the police.

Jason explained to the officer that he had seen Ezra earlier in the day and she wasn't acting like herself. He said his time in the military had heightened his awareness during situations like this and he was just concerned for her safety.

Police officers spoke briefly to Ezra and Alex as well, who both reassured them that there was no problem. Everything was fine. Just after 1:00 p.m., police left the house and Jason rode his bike back to Racy's Coffee Shop.

———

At 4:15 that afternoon, Don Sipple, who lived on a rural dairy farm twelve miles from Eau Claire, answered a knock on his door to find Ezra McCandless crying and shivering. She was barefoot and bruised, covered with mud and blood. Her pants and sweater were torn and she told him she needed a doctor.

When Don called 911, he told the operator that a young lady had come to his door and said she was attacked and needed help. She couldn't remember her own name, had no recollection of who attacked her, and had no idea how she got there. She had walked to the house but was unaware of where she had walked from.

When police and paramedics arrived and questioned her, Ezra's only recollection was that of being cold, scared, and her feet hurting. It seemed as if she was in shock. She was crying uncontrollably, bleeding lightly from the edges of her mouth, and had scratches on her body and the palm of her hand. When police asked if there was anyone she wanted them to call, she only gave one name: Jason Mengel.

When police spoke to Jason Mengel, he said he last saw Ezra with Alex Woodworth and told them of the incident earlier in the day, when the police were called. While doctors examined Ezra for injuries, police searched for Alex but he was nowhere to be found.

Alex's roommates hadn't seen him and his backpack, laptop, and things he would usually carry with him were still at his house. His cell phone was missing but there was no answer.

Alex was missing and the police couldn't locate Ezra's car either. Once doctors had determined that her injuries were minimal, detectives sat her down to try and find out what had happened that afternoon, as well as where Alex was. Her only explanation, however, was that her mind had blocked out the day's events.

Ezra explained the timeline of the day as she remembered. She told police that after Jason left, she and Alex had driven somewhere to talk. She said she wanted to go to a park to talk but her brain started to fizzle after that. She couldn't remember anything other than Alex getting upset with her because she was still talking to Jason.

Ezra had mentioned wanting to talk to Alex in a park, so police began their searches there. First, they checked all the local parks in the area but there was no sign of Alex or Ezra's car.

The following day, detectives began backtracking the possible routes to Don Sipple's home to figure out which way she had come from when she arrived at his house on foot.

About 300 yards from the entrance to the Sipple farm, they found an access to a muddy field where they could see fresh footprints in the mud. They followed the footprints until they reached the peak of a small hill; as officers crested the hill, they found Ezra's car. It was stuck in the mud.

As they got closer to the car, they knew they had found Alex Woodworth. The rear driver's side door was open and his bloody body was hanging from the vehicle near the rear wheel well.

The inside of the car was bloody but the ground around the outside was much bloodier. Alex's cell phone was found in the field, away from the car. Someone had removed the battery and smashed the phone to bits.

———

When police went back to tell Ezra that they had found her car and the body of Alex Woodworth, she suddenly remembered what had happened. She told detectives that Alex had become angry with her and tried to stab her, but she managed to wrangle the knife from him by grabbing the blade.

She showed police her left arm where the word "Boy" had been scratched into her forearm. According to Ezra, she and Alex were arguing in the car's front seat when he grabbed her arm and carved the word into her arm. She said she often called her "*my* boy." He meant it as a derogatory term to make fun of her struggle with her gender identity.

However, the problem with her story was her explanation of how Alex had carved it into her arm. If Alex had been in the driver's seat, as she had claimed, it would have been an awkward and unnatural position for him to carve it into her left arm at that angle.

Another problem with her story was the cut marks on her palm, where she claimed she had grabbed the knife blade as Alex tried to stab her. The wounds on her hands were simply surface scratches that needed no treatment at all, not even a band-aid. If she had grabbed the blade with enough force to wrench it away from him, the sharp edge would have torn her palms to shreds. It just didn't add up and the detectives knew it.

The rips on her pants presented yet another problem with her story. She claimed she struggled with Alex as he tried to cut her pants off. However, the cut marks on the pants were all vertical straight lines up and down the pant legs. The cut marks would have been much more random if there had been a struggle. The shreds on her pants were also all within arm's length, as if they had been self-inflicted.

Once again, Ezra changed her story. She now said that the attack had happened in the car's back seat and admitted that she had carved the word "Boy" into her arm herself. But that story didn't add up, either. Most of the blood was outside the car. From the footprints around the car, investigators could tell that the struggle had taken place outside the vehicle.

Alex had very few defensive wounds, leading investigators to believe he was ambushed with the first blow to the back of his head while inside the rear of the vehicle. When he got outside the car, she continued stabbing him in the head, neck, groin, and torso. The trail of blood and the vast amount of blood pooling were outside the car. He had been stabbed a total of sixteen times and his genitals were mutilated.

The knife, which had been a gift to Ezra from her stepfather, had been thrown into a ditch on the side of the road near Don Sipple's farmhouse.

All of Ezra McCandless' wounds were superficial but Alex Woodworth had been stabbed sixteen times. Her description of events didn't make sense. If the attack happened as she claimed, she could have run from him after any of the stab wounds. She would have had plenty of time to escape. Instead, she continued stabbing.

————

Two weeks after the incident, Ezra McCandless was arrested and charged with first-degree intentional homicide. She pleaded not guilty and claimed she had killed him in self-defense.

————

Eighteen months later, Ezra McCandless went on trial for murder. In court, she looked completely different. Her boyish demeanor was gone. She had removed the hoop that usually dangled from her septum and looked much more feminine in pink and pastel-colored floral prints. Her hair had grown longer and had been styled and at times she appeared timid and meek.

At other moments during the trial, she appeared to be joking and relaxed, calm and cool. Often smiling, she even showed off her outfits to her mother. One of her childhood friends mentioned to television news reporters that she seemed to light up when she took the stand in her own defense.

Ezra told the court that Alex Woodworth was into BDSM and was violent during sex; she feared for her life. She claimed that she had Alex's cell phone as she left the crime scene, but she fell and broke the phone, leaving her unable to call for help. When the jury was shown photos of the cell phone, however, it was damaged far worse than what a fall would create. It was obvious she had smashed the phone to pieces. Her true intent was to leave Alex with no means of calling for help.

The fact that Ezra had only superficial scratches that could have easily been self-inflicted, while Alex had been stabbed sixteen times, weighed heavily on the jury's decision. The forensic evidence had told a completely different story than what Ezra had told the police and the jury. Ultimately, Ezra's efforts to save herself from prison didn't succeed and, on November 1, 2019, after three hours of deliberation, the jury found her guilty.

Three months later, at her sentencing, Ezra McCandless looked like a different person than she did at trial. Her hair was cut short and matted down around her head. She wore no makeup or pastel colors this time: only an orange jump-suit and a sad face. She cried and told the judge that she loved Alex. She said she felt a great loss with his death and apologized to his family for what she had done.

Ezra McCandless was sentenced to life in prison with a minimum of fifty years. She will be more than seventy years old when she is eligible for parole.

CHAPTER 13
BONUS CHAPTER:
WORLD'S WORST MOM

This chapter is a **free bonus chapter** from True Crime Case Histories: Volume 9

———

In June 1984, Maybel Harrison drove along California State Route 89, northwest of Lake Tahoe, as the first hints of sunrise began to glow against the Sierra Nevada mountains. As she passed the Squaw Valley ski resort, she saw bright yellow flashes through the trees on the side of the road. Something was burning. Curious, she stopped the car and climbed down the sloped roadside to get a closer look. What she saw horrified her. A body was burning on top of what seemed to be a makeshift funeral pyre.

Maybel ran back to the highway and flagged down a trucker, who used his CB radio to alert the Placer County Sheriff. When authorities arrived and extinguished the fire, they found the body of a young woman burning on top of a heap of clothing and miscellaneous personal items. The woman appeared to be about twenty years old. Her legs and arms were bound and duct tape covered her mouth. Her body was almost entirely charred. Her cheeks and the backs of her calves were the only parts of her body that hadn't been burned.

In the heap beneath her body, investigators found pieces of clothing, jewelry, and a toothbrush but no identification at all. The body and the clothing had all been soaked with gasoline. Investigators were puzzled, however, when disposable diapers were found at the scene. There was no sign of a baby and an autopsy later revealed that the woman had never given birth.

Further examinations of the body showed that the girl had been severely abused over a long period of time and there was a large puncture wound on her back. However, neither the wound nor the abuse had killed her. The woman's lungs were filled with soot, indicating that she had been alive when she was set on fire, but it wasn't the fire that had killed her. She had died of smoke inhalation. Investigators searched dental records and examined what was left of her fingerprints, but there was simply no record of the girl.

A composite drawing was created based on what was left of her face and released to the media, but months went by without any clues as to her identity. From that point forward, the girl was only known as Jane Doe #4858-84.

———

Eleven months later, just six miles from where the first Jane Doe was found, a man walking in the Martis Creek Campground noticed a large box in some bushes not far from the road. When curiosity compelled him to open the box, he found the body of another young girl.

Again, investigators found no identification at the scene and no missing person reports matched her description. The second girl had died of dehydration and starvation. She, too, showed signs of severe abuse. The second girl became known as Jane Doe #6607-85.

Although the bodies were found near each other, the second body was found across county lines in a different jurisdiction and the two cases were not connected. It would be almost a decade before anyone would come forward with any information about the two murders.

––––––––

More than eight years had passed since the two bodies were found and twenty-three-year-old Terry Knorr's horrific secrets had eaten at her for as long as she could remember. She needed to tell someone. Anyone that would listen. But when Terry told Utah police what she knew, they brushed her off. So did her therapist. It was an insane story. It couldn't possibly be true.

In late October 1993, Terry Knorr called 1-800-CRIME-TV, the phone number for the television show America's Most Wanted. She knew they would listen. The TV show operators put her in contact with detectives in Placer County, California, where the first body had been found. Finally, she had found someone that took her seriously.

Terry shared with detectives her lifetime of horrific abuse at the hands of her sadistic mother, which led to the death of her two sisters, Suesan and Sheila Knorr. In less than a month after her phone call, the two Jane Does had been positively identified as her sisters and authorities had arrested her two brothers and her mother, Theresa Knorr.

———

Theresa Knorr was born Theresa Cross in 1946 to Jim and Swannie Cross. By her early teenage years, Theresa's father had developed Parkinson's disease and was no longer able to work, leaving her mother to raise the family. Theresa was very close to her mother. When she was just fifteen, however, while Theresa was buying groceries with her mother, Swannie Cross collapsed and died in her arms.

Her mother's death hit Theresa hard. With her father unable to work, the family had no income and were forced to sell the home they had lived in. Theresa fell into a deep depression and grasped for anyone to love her. At just sixteen years old, she dropped out of high school and married her first boyfriend, twenty-one-year-old Clifford Sanders.

Ten months after their wedding, Theresa gave birth to her first son, Howard Sanders. Their young marriage, however, was already having trouble. Theresa suffered relentless mood swings. One minute she would be a kind and loving wife, the next moment she was angry and accusatory. She complained that Clifford drank far too much and was insistent that he was having sex with women he had met in bars. In June 1964, after Clifford spent a night out drinking with friends, Theresa berated him when he finally returned home. The argument that ensued resulted in Clifford punching her in the face. Theresa reported the assault to the police but refused to press charges against her husband. Perhaps she had second thoughts – or another plan.

Less than a month later, Clifford spent his birthday out with friends rather than home with Theresa, who was now pregnant with their second child. Early the next morning, July 6, 1964, she confronted him and again accused him of infidelity. Clifford responded to the accusation by saying what had been on his mind for quite some time. He wanted a divorce. The news was more than she could take. Theresa flew into a jealous rage, grabbed a rifle, and shot him as he walked out of the back door.

Clifford had raised his hand to deflect the shot, but the bullet pierced his wrist, entered through his chest, and continued directly into his heart. It killed him instantly. At just eighteen, Theresa was charged with the murder of her husband.

During her murder trial, Theresa testified that Clifford Sanders was an abusive alcoholic and she had killed him in self-defense. She cried as she told the court that she had grabbed the gun only intending to threaten him. She only wanted him to stop hitting her. She claimed the gun had accidentally fired.

Although there was no evidence of bruising or other signs of physical abuse on her body as she had claimed, as well as an autopsy of Clifford's body that revealed there was no alcohol in his system at the time of his death, the jury couldn't say no to the poor, young, pregnant girl. She was acquitted. After the trial, several of the jurors came up to her and hugged her, expressing their satisfaction that she was finally rid of "that horrible man."

The day after her acquittal, Theresa brazenly showed up at the District Attorney's office, demanding they return the rifle that had been used as evidence against her.

The following March, Theresa gave birth to her second child, Sheila, and began dating Robert Knorr, a Marine Corps private. Knorr had done a tour in Vietnam where he was shot on two different occasions and had also a bridge blown up beneath him. The three incidents left him with severe injuries that had required several months of recovery in a military hospital.

Within months of meeting Robert Knorr, Theresa was pregnant again. On July 9, 1966, she and Robert Knorr were married. That September she gave birth to her third child, Suesan Knorr, and the couple had two more boys in quick succession, William and Robert Jr. Knorr.

Due to his injuries in Vietnam, Robert Knorr's subsequent job opportunities with the military were limited. Restricted to light duty, he was assigned as a funeral escort which required travel all over the country. When young men returned from Vietnam in body bags, Robert Knorr was there to carry a casket or shoot a rifle into the air as part of a twenty-one gun salute.

With her husband gone for several days at a time, it left Theresa home to take care of five children. Again, her imagination went wild. Like she did with her first husband, Theresa accused Robert of infidelity.

As her anger festered, Theresa aimed her aggression at her children, abusing them physically, verbally, and psychologically. By late 1969, Theresa was pregnant a sixth time but her marriage with Robert was collapsing quickly. She was prone to frequent outbursts of anger and accusations and Robert couldn't take another day of what was to become the onset of her borderline personality disorder. With Theresa seven months pregnant, the two divorced in June 1970.

Two months after the divorce was finalized, Theresa gave birth to a girl, Terry. However, when Robert came to visit the children, she refused to allow him access. From that point on, Robert was no longer allowed to see his children.

The following year, Theresa Knorr married once again. This time, however, the accusations of infidelity flew from both her and her new husband from the very beginning. They were divorced within a year.

Theresa spent the next four years drinking at the American Legion Hall in Rio Linda, California, and often left her children home alone for days at a time. In August 1976, she met and married Chet Harris after having known each other for only three days. Chet was almost thirty years older than Theresa. Although she quickly grew to hate him, he and her daughter, Suesan, grew close, which angered her even more. After less than four months of marriage, she had divorced once again.

The final divorce changed Theresa dramatically. She drank more and more, gained a tremendous amount of weight, and became increasingly anti-social – so much so that she got rid of the telephone as she didn't want to speak to anyone and wouldn't even allow the children to have friends over. Unfortunately, the change that the children noticed most was at the level of abuse. To Theresa, the children were the spawn of the devil, Robert Knorr, so they deserved to be punished.

As her level of drinking escalated, so too did her mania. She often threw kitchen knives or scissors at the children and once put a gun to the head of her youngest daughter, Terry, as she threatened to kill her. Beatings occurred almost daily. The children were burned with cigarettes and force-fed until the point of vomiting. When they vomited, she made them eat that too. Theresa ordered her children to hold the others down when it was time for a beating, with the boys often ordered to participate in the beating of their siblings or face a beating themselves.

The girls received the bulk of the abuse, especially Suesan. Theresa's delusions grew more and more insane. She truly believed her girls were demons. As Theresa got older, fatter, and uglier, the young girls, reaching their teenage years, became more beautiful. Theresa, who had once been young and attractive, was convinced the girls had cast a spell on her: they were stealing her beauty and causing her to gain weight.

Howard, the oldest son, was the lucky one. He managed to get away from the madness. He left home when the family moved to a run-down trailer park on Auburn Boulevard in Sacramento in 1983, just before the real insanity began.

The new neighborhood was known for seedy motels, street prostitution, heroin addicts, and drug dealers. But even in a neighborhood like that, the Knorr family stood out. Neighbors noticed that their two-bedroom apartment smelled of urine and the children were rarely let outside of the house.

In 1980, fifteen-year-old Suesan Knorr was picked up on the streets of Sacramento. She had run away from home and was trying to survive as a prostitute. Suesan was caught by a truancy officer and placed in a psychiatric hospital. In the hospital, she told of the extreme abuse that she had received from her mother. However, when authorities confronted her mother, Theresa denied any accusations of abuse. The other children backed up their mother's lie, knowing they would be beaten if they didn't. Theresa assured authorities that Suesan had mental problems and often made up crazy stories. Without further investigation, Suesan was returned to the custody of her mother.

Scared to death, Suesan returned home and prepared for the worst. Theresa donned heavy leather gloves to protect her fists as she punished her daughter with a brutal beating. Suesan's siblings were all ordered to take part in the beating as well, passing around the leather gloves until they were covered with Suesan's blood.

For her defiance, Suesan was handcuffed beneath the kitchen table and the other children were ordered to watch over her to make sure she didn't escape. From that point on, none of the children ever went to school again. Theresa had told their previous school that they had moved out of the school district but never bothered to enroll the children in a new school. Most of them never made it past the eighth grade.

Suesan was kept secured under the table for the next two years. The gag in her mouth was only occasionally removed when her mother hand-fed her. When Suesan rebelled, she was force-fed to the point of vomiting. Theresa, of course, made her eat that too. By 1982, Suesan's will had broken and her mother removed her handcuffs. She was finally allowed to sleep with the other children.

Despite her abuse, Suesan was still the only child that had been brave enough to stand up to their mother – but her defiance continually made her a target. During an argument in June 1983, Theresa flew into a manic rage and ordered her sons to hold Suesan still while she pulled out a gun and shot her daughter in the chest.

Suesan slumped and bled out on the floor, but she was still alive. Barely. The bullet had missed any vital organs but had lodged in her spine. Theresa ordered the children to handcuff Suesan and lay her in the bathtub, where she stayed for almost two months as her mother nursed her back to health. The children were ordered to tell no one.

Miraculously, Suesan recovered. When she was well enough, Suesan begged her mother to let her leave the home to make a life on her own and, surprisingly, Theresa agreed. But her freedom would come with one stipulation – she needed to have the bullet in her spine removed. Theresa didn't want there to be any evidence that she had shot her daughter.

In July 1984, Theresa Knorr prepared for an amateur surgery in the home. She gave Suesan a heavy dose of Thioridazine (a drug to treat schizophrenia) and a bottle of whiskey, then had her lay on the kitchen table. The drug and alcohol cocktail knocked Suesan unconscious and the surgery began.

Theresa handed her son, Robert Jr., an X-Acto knife and ordered him to dig into her back to look for the bullet. Robert dug deep into his sister's back with the knife and probed with his fingers to find and remove the bullet. The surgery was a success. But, when Suesan finally woke, her pain was excruciating. Theresa fed her antibiotics and ibuprofen to ease the pain but they only seemed to make her condition worse. Within days, Suesan's eyes had turned yellow and she was no longer able to control her bowels. Internal bleeding caused massive black bruises on her back. Suesan then slipped into a coma.

On July 16, 1984, Theresa filled plastic garbage bags with all of Suesan's belongings. Every piece of clothing she owned, every photo of her, anything that proved she ever existed went into the garbage bags. She then ordered William and Robert Jr. to put a diaper on their sister, duct tape her mouth shut, and carry her to the trunk of the car.

The family left Sacramento with Suesan in the trunk and drove east until they reached Highway 89. They drove south through the night along Highway 89 and pulled over near the banks of Square Creek. Theresa carried the garbage bags with Suesan's belongings to an area near the creek bed while the boys carried their sister and laid her on top of the trash bags. Theresa then doused her daughter and her belongings with gasoline, lit a match, and walked away.

————

It didn't take long before all the anger and insanity that had been directed at Suesan was directed at Sheila. Theresa had been drawing unemployment but found a new way to supplement her income: she forced twenty-year-old Sheila onto the streets into a life of prostitution.

Life as a prostitute horrified Sheila, but it seemed to please Theresa. The money Sheila brought home was much more than her unemployment payments. As a result, Sheila was allowed to leave the house as she pleased for short periods of time and received fewer beatings.

But by May 1985, everything changed. Theresa contracted a sexually transmitted disease – worse, she believed she caught it from using the toilet after Sheila. She also accused Sheila of allowing herself to get pregnant during her sex work.

Sheila was gagged, her feet were bound, and her hands were tied behind her back. Theresa, William, and Robert Jr. beat Sheila within inches of her life. They then placed her into a small linen closet measuring only sixteen inches by twenty-four inches. The shelving of the closet made it even smaller. There was only room for her to stand. She couldn't kneel, sit, or even turn around. Though the children could hear grunting and moans coming from the closet, they were strictly forbidden to open the door under any circumstances. No food, no water, no bathroom. Nothing. When the noises coming from the closet got too loud, Theresa would just turn up the television.

After three days in the closet, the family heard a loud thud. Still, Theresa insisted that none of the children open the closet door. After another three days, however, the smell was too much to stand. When they opened the door, Sheila's decomposing body was curled up on the floor. She had died of starvation and dehydration.

———

Theresa filled a large cardboard box with blankets and the boys placed Sheila's body into the box. They then put the box in the trunk and again drove through the night toward Lake Tahoe. Theresa instructed the boys to dump the box next to some bushes near the banks of a small lake in Martis Creek Campground. Just a few hours after they dumped her body, a man found the box and alerted the police.

———

For the next three months, the family could still smell the unmistakable odor of decomposition lingering in the house. Theresa was convinced that the smell alone could implicate her in the death of her daughter. On September 29, 1986, the family packed their belongings and moved out. However, sixteen-year-old Terry was ordered to go back to the apartment, douse it in lighter fluid, and set it on fire. She did as she was told, but the three containers of lighter fluid weren't enough to do much damage. Neighbors quickly called the fire department and most of the apartment was left intact, including the closet where Sheila had died.

Terry knew that she would be the next target of her mother's rage – both of her sisters had warned her. Rather than go into hiding with her mother and brothers, Terry ran away. She had kept Sheila's identification card and spent the next several years posing as her sister.

After leaving the Sacramento home, twenty-four-year-old William also cut ties with his mother and moved in with his girlfriend. Robert Jr. stuck by his mother's side and the two of them moved to Las Vegas.

Robert Jr. and Theresa Knorr kept a low profile in Las Vegas for years until November 7, 1991, when Robert attempted to rob a bar and ended up killing the bartender. He was convicted of murder and sentenced to sixteen years in prison. Immediately after her son's arrest, Theresa moved to Salt Lake City, Utah, where she started using her maiden name and got a job as a caregiver for an elderly woman.

———

Almost nine years had passed since Sheila's death when Terry Knorr and her new husband decided to call the America's Most Wanted hotline.

When Terry told police the horrific story, they revisited the evidence recovered from both of the Jane Doe scenes. Fingerprints were lifted from the box in which Sheila's body had been discovered. The prints matched both William and Robert Jr. The box was traced back to a movie theater where William had once worked.

William Knorr was still living in the Sacramento area and worked in a warehouse when he was arrested. When questioned, he initially denied everything. However, when detectives laid out the evidence against him, his brother, and his mother, he admitted his guilt. Robert Jr. was brought from his prison cell in Nevada back to California to face charges. He, too, initially denied involvement but later admitted his guilt.

Theresa Knorr had been tracked down via a driver's license application she had filed in Utah. Just five days before her arrest, she had been arrested for driving under the influence of alcohol. When officers showed up at the address on her driver's license, she was already packing her bags. She knew the police were looking for her. When questioned by detectives, she refused to cooperate and immediately requested legal counsel.

Theresa Knorr was charged with two counts of murder, two counts of conspiracy to commit murder, and two special circumstances charges: multiple murder and murder by torture. She initially pleaded not guilty but later changed her plea when she was told that her son, William, was planning to testify against her. Her guilty plea eliminated the chance that she would be sentenced to death.

On October 17, 1995, Theresa Knorr was sentenced to two consecutive life sentences. She will be eligible for parole in 2027 at the age of eighty.

Although the boys had pleaded guilty, the circumstances of their involvement in the murders of their siblings were not cut and dry. Their lifetime of abuse and constant threat of further abuse clearly influenced their involvement.

For his role in the murders, William Knorr was sentenced to probation and ordered to undergo psychological therapy. Robert Knorr Jr. received an additional three years concurrent to his existing prison sentence for the bartender's murder. After his release from prison, Robert Jr. was arrested again in 2014 on multiple child pornography charges. He is due to be released in 2024.

Terry Knorr died of a fatal heart attack in 2011. She was forty-one years old.

————

This chapter is a free bonus chapter from True Crime Case Histories: Volume 9

Online Appendix

Visit my website for additional photos and videos pertaining to the cases in this book:

http://TrueCrimeCaseHistories.com/vol10/

More books by Jason Neal

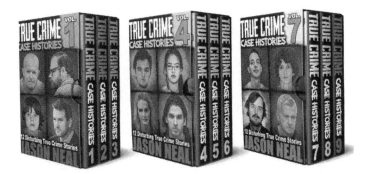

Looking for more?? I am constantly adding new volumes of True Crime Case Histories. The series **can be read in any order,** and all books are available in paperback, hardcover, and audiobook.

Check out the complete series at:

https://amazon.com/author/jason-neal

All Jason Neal books are also available in **AudioBook format at Audible.com.** Enjoy a **Free Audiobook** when you signup for a 30-Day trial using this link:

https://geni.us/AudibleTrueCrime

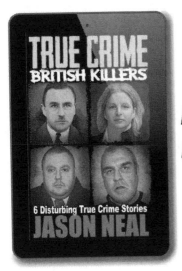

FREE BONUS EBOOK FOR MY READERS

As my way of saying "Thank you" for downloading, I'm giving away a FREE True Crime e-book I think you'll enjoy.

https://TrueCrimeCaseHistories.com

Just visit the link above to let me know where to send your free book!

THANK YOU!

Thank you for reading this Volume of True Crime Case Histories. I truly hope you enjoyed it. If you did, I would be sincerely grateful if you would take a few minutes to write a review for me on Amazon using the link below.

https://geni.us/TrueCrime10

I'd also like to encourage you to sign-up for my email list for updates, discounts, and freebies on future books! I promise I'll make it worth your while with future freebies.

http://truecrimecasehistories.com

And please take a moment and follow me on Amazon.

One last thing. As I mentioned previously, many of the stories in this series were suggested to me by readers like you. I like to feature stories that many true crime fans haven't heard of, so if there's a story that you remember from the past that you haven't seen covered by other true crime sources, please send me any details you can remember and I will do my best to research it. Or if you'd like to contact me for any other reason free to email me at:

jasonnealbooks@gmail.com

https://linktr.ee/JasonNeal

Thanks so much,

Jason Neal

ABOUT THE AUTHOR

Jason Neal is a Best-Selling American True Crime Author living in Hawaii with his Turkish-British wife. Jason started his writing career in the late eighties as a music industry publisher and wrote his first true crime collection in 2019.

As a boy growing up in the eighties just south of Seattle, Jason became interested in true crime stories after hearing the news of the Green River Killer so close to his home. Over the subsequent years he would read everything he could get his hands on about true crime and serial killers.

As he approached 50, Jason began to assemble stories of the crimes that have fascinated him most throughout his life. He's especially obsessed by cases solved by sheer luck, amazing police work, and groundbreaking technology like early DNA cases and more recently reverse genealogy.